The Wilderness Within You

By the same author

THE WILDERNESS WITHIN YOU

A Lenten journey with Jesus,
deep in conversation

Penelope Wilcock

MONARCH
BOOKS
Oxford, UK & Grand Rapids, Michigan, USA

Published by Monarch Books
an imprint of
Lion Hudson plc
Wilkinson House, Jordan Hill Road,
Oxford OX2 8DR, England
Email: monarch@lionhudson.com
www.lionhudson.com/monarch

ISBN 978 0 85721 497 3
e-ISBN 978 0 85721 498 0

First edition 2013

Acknowledgments
Scripture quotations marked NIV taken from the Holy Bible, New International
Version Anglicised. Copyright © 1979, 1984, 2011 Biblica, formerly International
Bible Society. Used by permission of Hodder & Stoughton Ltd, an Hachette UK
company. All rights reserved. "NIV" is a registered trademark of Biblica. UK
trademark number 1448790. Scripture quotations marked KJV taken from The
Authorized (King James) Version. Rights in the Authorized Version are vested
in the Crown. Reproduced by permission of the Crown's patentee, Cambridge
University Press. Scripture quotations marked RSV are from The Revised
Standard Version of the Bible copyright © 1346, 1952 and 1971 by the Division
of Christian Education of the National Council of Churches in the USA. Used
by permission. All Rights Reserved. Scripture quotations marked NRSV are from
The New Revised Standard Version of the Bible copyright © 1989 by the Division
of Christian Education of the National Council of Churches in the USA. Used by
permission. All Rights Reserved. Scripture quotations marked The Message taken
from The Message. Copyright © by Eugene H. Peterson 1993, 1994, 1995, 1996,
2000, 2001, 2002. Used by permission of NavPress Publishing Group. Scriptures
quotations marked GNT are from the Good News Bible © 1994 published by the
Bible Societies/HarperCollins Publishers Ltd UK, Good News Bible© American
Bible Society 1966, 1971, 1976, 1992. Used with permission.

A catalogue record for this book is available from the British Library

Printed and bound in the UK, October 2013, LH26

To Tony Collins,

my first and best editor,

my beloved husband,

and my dearest friend

Author's note

This is a work of fiction. None of the persons and events in Silverhill and the surrounding area described herein bear any resemblance to any person in real life.

Contents

"Heaven and earth will pass away, but my words will never pass away."

(Jesus of Nazareth; Mark 13:31 NIV)

Day 1

Ash Wednesday

Luke 14:26–27, 33 NIV

"If anyone comes to me and does not hate father and mother, wife and children, brothers and sisters – yes, even their own life – such a person cannot be my disciple. And whoever does not carry their cross and follow me cannot be my disciple...

"... In the same way, those of you who do not give up everything you have cannot be my disciples."

I have so many questions. Life is not easy when you have a literalistic mind. It becomes hard to know what people mean. When I take them literally they get angry, find me obtuse, provocative. They expect me to know what they mean. I expect them to say what they mean. But meaning in the speech of most people is complicated and metaphorical, hard for me to get to. Nowhere is this more true than in religion.

"Those of you who do not give up everything you have cannot be my disciples," says Jesus. I stick on that. What does he mean?

Does he mean what I would mean if I said that? Does he mean, "Give away the car and go on foot or by bus. Give away all your ornaments and memorabilia. Have by you only a small selection of plain and modest clothes, a mattress to lie on at night, a set of shelves, some sturdy sandals, a few spiritual classics, the tools of your trade and a comb"?

I ask around. What does Jesus mean? Friends assure me that

Jesus did not mean what he said, exactly. They tell me he means you must not be attached to your possessions, but must prioritize the things of the spirit. Irritated by my literalism as I persist, they point out the educational value of owning a TV, the modern necessity of cars. A body has to eat, they remind me, and it's cheaper to bake your own bread, brew your own coffee – hence the kitchen gadgets. Jesus calls us to love one another – hence the family photographs and large wedding celebrations, the lengthy Christmas present list, the holidays abroad to spend quality time together – after all, Jesus also said we should get away from it all together from time to time.

They point out that Jesus is as much for the rich as for the poor, that the soul is measured not by income and possessions (or lack of them) but by whether God has first place in that person's heart. And then I want to ask, if God has first place – isn't that enough? Are all these other things necessary? And if they aren't, why bother with all this repair and maintenance – not to mention the electronic gates and the contents insurance?

I fall silent. In my childhood, I learned to read the warning in a tone of voice, and I recognize that my questions are not welcome. But still I am left wondering: if he didn't mean what he said, which is what I think he meant, what did he mean? It doesn't *sound* metaphorical. What does he want me to do? Me, in daily life? How am I to live, if all they can tell me is he meant something other than what he said?

Senses shift and change. I attend carefully to what is said about other parts of the Bible. Some are taken literally, and said to be eternal; others are supposed to be interpreted loosely or ignored completely – like the warnings against usury, on which modern society is based.

"Whoever does not carry their cross and follow me cannot be my disciple," he said. This worries me. I am afraid of growing old, of running out of money, of my own inadequacy and incompetence, my social ineptitude. These are enough to worry about. I know, for a surety, I cannot cope with the notion of crucifixion. The things human beings do to each other drives me crazy. My mind dissolves in horror at the prospect of torture. I am sickened by war, revolted by the corruption of power and what it does to people. A *cross*? Does he mean that?

"I am the way and the truth and the life," says Jesus. "No one comes to the Father except through me" (John 14:6 NIV).

This means that unless I follow Jesus, I am cut adrift in this world, lost and without hope. But I cannot follow Jesus without being crucified. I stand dithering. I have so many questions. It feels like being stuck in a maze; what looks like a way turns out to be a cul-de-sac, and nothing leads anywhere. I feel like someone who intended a nature walk in the country but walked too far off the track and unfortunately neglected to bring a map. In this wilderness there are no comforting Heritage signs with a helpful arrow to tell me, "YOU ARE HERE." I mean, I know I am here – but where?

And then I make a decision. Jesus, they say, went into the wilderness. Yes, he rose from the dead and ascended into heaven – but that comes later in the story. I'm going to begin it where I am, and look for him here.

My hope is that among all the tangling briars and inhospitable undergrowth of my inner landscape, I will turn a corner somewhere and find him. And when I do, I am going to ask him all these questions that are tormenting me, pushing me around until I feel completely bewildered. So many. And I have one big question that almost hurts in my heart because I care about the answer so much. I want to ask him, "Jesus, what do you think of me?"

Day 2

Thursday of Week 1

Deuteronomy 2:1–8, 26–29 NIV

Then we turned back and set out towards the wilderness along the route to the Red Sea, as the Lord had directed me. For a long time we made our way around the hill country of Seir.

Then the Lord said to me, "You have made your way around this hill country long enough; now turn north. Give the people these orders: 'You are about to pass through the territory of your relatives the descendants of Esau, who live in Seir. They will be afraid of you, but be very careful. Do not provoke them to war, for I will not give you any of their land, not even enough to put your foot on. I have given Esau the hill country of Seir as his own. You are to pay them in silver for the food you eat and the water you drink.'"

The Lord your God has blessed you in all the work of your hands. He has watched over your journey through this vast wilderness. These forty years the Lord your God has been with you, and you have not lacked anything.

So we went on past our relatives the descendants of Esau, who live in Seir. We turned from the Arabah road, which comes up from Elath and Ezion Geber, and travelled along the desert road of Moab...

... From the Desert of Kedemoth I sent messengers to Sihon king of Heshbon offering peace and saying, "Let us pass through your country. We will stay on the main road; we will not turn aside to the right or to the left. Sell us food to eat and water to drink for their price in silver. Only let us pass through on foot – as the

descendants of Esau, who live in Seir, and the Moabites, who live in Ar, did for us – until we cross the Jordan into the land the Lord our God is giving us."

I stand at the traffic lights, waiting to cross. I'll tell you now, this junction is insane. From this side of the road, leaving the supermarket with our plastic bags full of cheap food, we stand waiting for the little green man to show up, because the cars and buses and lorries seem to come from everywhere. Across the road from me, in the rain, I watch a man waiting patiently for the green man to light up, and he has what? Motor neurone disease, maybe? A longstanding spinal problem? Supported by crutches, his useless feet dragging hopelessly in their orthopaedic shoes, he waits. Once the light changes he has two car lanes, a bus lane, and a layby to make it over before he reaches the far side in safety. He can only go slowly. Brave. I pass him on my way over.

We stand in the next island, jostled together like herded sheep in a pen. Two more car lanes to cross before the next crossing place. And after that, two more, and then a single lane. All controlled by lights – pedestrians meekly obeying automata because it is safe to do nothing else; everything goes so fast and it's so easy to make a mistake.

Standing in this tarmac and concrete jungle, where instead of tree trunks a forest of telegraph poles, belisha beacons, traffic lights, street signs, and lamp posts has sprung up, I wonder about wilderness. How far from all this would Jesus be found? That man of the hills, his gaze adjusted to the expanses of the sea of Galilee, his footfall to the dusty tracks where sheep follow and camels gather by the well.

The lights (wouldn't you know it) are not synchronized. Every time our little pedestrian huddle swishes across in its anoraks through the downpour, we stop again. The lights are against us every time. As we wait for the beeping to begin that will trigger our obedient forward surge, I reflect upon the meaning of civilization. Do we *belong* here? The human race, I mean. Were we born for this? In this urban wasteland, trained to compliance, our movements conditioned by fear in so many ways, do we really live? Or are we just passing through, paying our way on a trail to nowhere, some promised land that looks more like a mirage every day? What does it mean, in real terms, "civilization"?

It is at the last crossing that, for all the moisture in the air, my mouth goes dry and my heart misses a beat. Nobody looks up in the urban landscape. As I stand with my eyes trained to the ground, I become unexpectedly aware that I am looking at sandals. The person – a man – next to me on the traffic island is wearing sandals. And a homespun robe that reaches down not quite to his ankles. As my gaze travels dumbfounded upward, adrenalin sparkles through my every cell. My hair moves on my scalp. A feeling like water trickles the length of my spine. Because I know who this is. And apparently – a quick, wild glance round tells me this – nobody else can see him.

When my eyes meet his eyes – the gaze I have yearned for so long to find, to link in with, to search – my mind has just enough elastic left in it to frame the obvious question: "What… what are you doing here?"

His eyes are laughing. He looks at me, but he doesn't speak. But I understand him. This – here – the Silverhill traffic lights with the nightmare crossing; the dreary clot of rundown shops and grubby houses bathed in traffic fumes; the footsoldiering drifts of damp humanity slogging through the drizzle to find cheap supermarket deals and avoid colliding with vehicles of impatience – well, he includes this in his definition of "wilderness". And, yes – when I come to think of it, I believe I do too.

But if all this, that we have worked so hard to build and buy – the shops and houses, the food in plastic packets from the chain store, the river of cars endlessly streaming by – turns out to be no more than a wilderness we are passing through, what will be our destination? If this is not "home", what is?

That was our first meeting. Crossing the road.

Day 3

Friday of Week 1

Psalm 22:24 The Message

*He has never let you down, never looked the other way when
you were being kicked around.*
*He has never wandered off to do his own thing; he has been
right there, listening.*

Psalm 9:18–19 RSV

*For the needy shall not always be forgotten, and the hope of
the poor shall not perish for ever. Arise, O Lord! Let not man
prevail...*

Isaiah 7:14 NRSV

*Therefore the Lord himself will give you a sign. Look, the young
woman is with child and shall bear a son, and shall name him
Immanuel.*

Hebrews 13:1–6 NRSV

*Let mutual love continue. Do not neglect to show hospitality to
strangers, for by doing that some have entertained angels without
knowing it. Remember those who are in prison, as though you
were in prison with them; those who are being tortured, as
though you yourselves were being tortured. Let marriage be held
in honour by all, and let the marriage bed be kept undefiled; for
God will judge fornicators and adulterers. Keep your lives free
from the love of money, and be content with what you have; for*

*he has said, "I will never leave you or forsake you." So we can
say with confidence,*

*"The Lord is my helper; I will not be afraid. What can
anyone do to me?"*

I don't know when I will have this chance again – to ask the
questions that always bugged me, and not only hear his answers
but watch his response, read the look on his face. So there we
are – on this, the third day of Lent, I decide to go for broke
and ask him what everyone seems to want to know: "Why do
children die? Why do people suffer? Why does God just look on
and let rich and powerful people oppress the poor? Why does
God watch while children are abused and trafficked for sex?
Why doesn't he do something about it?"

And Jesus, having listened carefully to these questions, looks
up at me. His eyes can see right into my soul, and this seems
to go on for a very long time. And he asks me, "Are those your
questions or someone else's?"

It occurs to me that not only is there very little point trying
to mess Jesus around with half-truths and pretence, but it would
actually be extremely hard to do. No. I think I want to amend
"extremely hard" to "impossible". Especially when he's looking
at you.

"Well," I say, "those are the questions that I've heard people
asking time and time again. So I thought I'd take the chance to
find out what you really think. They are like the trump cards
people use in the game of believing – 'Ha ha! See? There is no
God!' And I thought you might be able to answer them."

He nods. "Yes," he says: "but they are not your own
questions?"

"No," I admit, "not really. When I hear them, what I think
is that *God* might as well ask *us* those things. I think he could
reasonably say, I gave you wealth and instead of sharing it fairly

you were greedy with it and wasted it – what do you think you were doing? Or, I entrusted into your care the most precious and beautiful gift of all, a little child – and you starved and beat her, neglected and abused her, raped and sold her: you cannot begin to imagine the wrath that will descend upon you personally and as a society because of this.

"Where there is inequality and oppression, wars come; in their wake is poverty and destruction. Where there is promiscuity, death and disease follows – I know it isn't politically correct to say so, but hey. Where people are selfish and neglect to care for the weaker members of their families, poverty, need, want, and sickness follow. Why blame God? And until people give up booze and fags and overeating, how can they possibly accuse God of not looking after them properly? It's like calling suicide murder.

"And I think that if you took away from the face of the earth every man-made problem, leaving only the natural disasters like tsunamis and cyclones and earthquakes and plagues, and if we set our energies and resources to work addressing and responding to those – why, the earth would be a paradise. And that was how God meant for it to be. A paradise with a few challenges, which he gave us the resources to fix. But we seem hell-bent on turning paradise to desert and wilderness, and holding God responsible for not stopping us. That's what I think."

Jesus' eyebrows twitch just a little, and a small grin tugs at the corners of his mouth. "I'm sorry," I say. "I suppose that was a bit of a rant. Anyway, that's what I think. What about you?"

"Well," says Jesus carefully, "cause and effect don't always show up in the same place. This person does a bad thing, and as a result that person suffers – but the first person doesn't care. And there are always reasons. There's a reason for everything, but that's not really the same as a solution. So long as people are free to act, the consequences will show up in everyone's life. And to take away freedom is oppression, which of itself causes suffering, as any slave can tell you. So what I did – call it what the Father did if you like, it comes to the same thing – is to share it. I wasn't ignoring it; that was my response. To go to the place where poverty and sorrow, sickness and pain, fear and grief, oppression and torture are, and do what I could. And because sometimes there were no options available for healing or changing the status quo, what happened to other people I allowed to be done to me. The thing is, an answer is not always framed in words. When it's really important, you don't send a message explaining – you go yourself."

Day 4

Saturday of Week 1

Psalm 69:1–3, 15–17 RSV

Save me, O God! For the waters have come up to my neck.
I sink in deep mire, where there is no foothold;
I have come into deep waters, and the flood sweeps over me.
I am weary with my crying; my throat is parched.
My eyes grow dim with waiting for my God…
… Let not the flood sweep over me,
or the deep swallow me up,
or the pit close its mouth over me.
Answer me, O Lord, for thy steadfast love is good;
according to thy abundant mercy, turn to me.
Hide not thy face from thy servant;
for I am in distress, make haste to answer me.

Psalm 88:6–7 RSV

Thou hast put me in the depths of the Pit, in the regions
dark and deep.
Thy wrath lies heavy upon me, and thou dost overwhelm
me with all thy waves.

Psalm 77:10 Common Worship

And I said, "My grief is this: that the right hand of the
Most High has lost its strength."

Isaiah 43:1–2 The Message

Don't be afraid, I've redeemed you. I've called your name.
You're mine.
When you're in over your head, I'll be there with you.

Mark 15:33–34 The Message

At noon the sky became extremely dark. The darkness lasted
three hours. At three o'clock, Jesus groaned out of the depths,
crying loudly, "Eloi, Eloi, lama sabachthani?" which means,
"My God, my God, why have you abandoned me?"

"Can I come back to you about something?" I ask him.

"Of course," says Jesus.

"Well, if you don't mind I want to push just a bit harder on something we were talking about yesterday. The thing is, when I'm listening to friends who are caught between a rock and a hard place, I can't help noticing that everything we normally say about God and humanity starts to sound like treacly platitudes. People don't want to hear that there is a pattern and a purpose in everything when their child in chemotherapy is throwing up stomach acid into a mouth full of sores. They aren't receptive to the news that God loves them when they stand at the graveside on a sweet summer day and watch the tiny white coffin of their stillborn baby lowered into the ground. It's not easy, you know? They get overwhelmed. Some of these guys have been to hell and back, if you know what I mean."

"Yes," he says softly. "Yes. I do know what you mean."

I pause on his comment, and register how odd it is to be speaking to the one individual in the entire history of humanity who can say that with no taint of inaccuracy.

"And you get people who are right in the thick of religion – clergy even – who could quote you most of Good Friday with the Book shut, and have spent thirty years talking about the foot of the cross; and then something happens – a man has to sit at the bedside and watch the slow, grim deterioration as his wife goes through mastectomy, radiotherapy, chemotherapy and all its poisonous devastation, then liver cancer, and at last death; and he just loses it all. His faith doesn't hold up. He gets overwhelmed. And you can tell him what you like then about how God has a plan and knows and loves us all and his wife is in a better place – and will he care?

"The rage of people in grief rails against God. That terrible mask of mourning in a river of tears is raised against a silent sky screaming, 'You let me down! How could you do this? Why have you abandoned me?' And what can you say – not you personally I mean; me, anyone – what words are there? What can reach them in that wilderness place?"

Jesus doesn't speak for a full minute. I feel the silence like a bubble of glass, brittle, fragile. I know he could in his own turn get angry right back. From the day he was born there was somebody out to kill him. Soldiers. Religious fanatics. Politicians indentured to expediency. The same old same old. The thorns, the spit, the spiked lash tearing up the skin of his back, the trembling struggle to carry his own cross through the streets of Jerusalem, crashing to his knees because it was too heavy, the nails hammering in, the thirst and yammering agony, no escape. What can you tell Jesus about what it is to feel abandoned?

"I hoped," he says quietly now, "the ones who are overwhelmed and in utter despair might find the God they are looking for in me. That's what it was all about. I can't alleviate wilderness, you know that. What I deal in is not the stuff of fairy tales – I have no magic wand. I can offer only truth, and I know all too well that truth sometimes agonizes you, breaks you. And as for the pattern, the purpose, well, yes, it's there – it is, truly. If you understand and can see it, it's there, and times when you can't understand and can't see it at all, it's still there. The same sun shines on the desert places as on the garden with its roses and fruit trees and lavender. In the desert it burns you because there is no escape from it. That's how it is."

I listen to his words, and I hope I will remember them when these astonishing days of walking close to him are over – because I know such times come and go; he will not always feel so near. Watching his face it is as though my heart is drawn out of my body, I love him so. This Jesus whom I do and do not follow, whom I adore but most of the time do not obey.

"I have in every case only one thing to offer, one answer," he says. "Just the same as I said yesterday. It's a promise. I am with you. Come hell or high water, I am with you."

He looks straight at me then. "I don't break my promises," he says.

Day 5

First Sunday in Lent

John 21:20–22 NIV

Peter turned and saw that the disciple whom Jesus loved was following them. (This was the one who had leaned back against Jesus at the supper and had said, "Lord, who is going to betray you?") When Peter saw him, he asked, "Lord, what about him?"

Jesus answered, "If I want him to remain alive until I return, what is that to you? You must follow me."

Mark 8:27–29 GNT

Then Jesus and his disciples went away to the villages near Caesarea Philippi. On the way he asked them, "Tell me, who do people say I am?"

"Some say that you are John the Baptist," they answered; "others say that you are Elijah, while others say that you are one of the prophets."

"What about you?" he asked them. "Who do you say I am?"

1 John 1:1–4 RSV
(taking alternate translation offered for verse 4)

That which was from the beginning, which we have heard, which we have seen with our eyes, which we have looked upon and touched with our hands, concerning the word of life — the life was made manifest, and we saw it, and testify to it, and proclaim to you the eternal life which was with the Father and

was made manifest to us – that which we have seen and heard
we proclaim also to you, so that you may have fellowship with
us; and our fellowship is with the Father and with his Son Jesus
Christ. And we are writing this that your joy may be complete.

This Lent is different for me from any other, because of spending time with Jesus. Walking along to church with him is not the same as going by myself – nor, for that matter is going to the grocery store or the bank or travelling on the bus. Walking by the sea with Jesus, and in the hills of the country park – it makes me see everything differently. And when I'm chilling out with family and friends, it feels like I have this great big secret – that I get to spend time with Jesus – I mean, how mind-blowing is that? You know that ice-breaker they sometimes have at meetings where you have to list the ten people from all time you would most like to invite for dinner? Of course people pick Gandhi and Martin Luther King, Jr and Mother Teresa (hmm – would she share your dinner or would you have to share hers?) and Shakespeare, and a few people further out along the branch want Svengali (can you have fictional people?) and Machiavelli and the Kray brothers and the Queen of Sheba, or Schoenberg and Buster Keaton. But nearly everyone wants to meet Jesus – or so they say – and I get to hang out with him every day. I mean, honestly – is that cool or is it cool?

And he came with me to church. He mixed right in, hugging everybody when it came to sharing the Peace, like we always do, and coming up with everyone else to receive the Eucharist: and how weird is that when you come to think about it? It is just mind-blowing. Exciting and hard to get my head round. Jesus! In our church! Imagine!

So walking home on this grey, chill day with the wind blowing up from the sea, I ask him: "What did you think?"

And Jesus smiles in a kind of enigmatic way that doesn't tell me a lot, which is a bit disappointing. So I try again, with more definite questions.

"What did you think of the sermon? Do you like the choir? How do you feel about all the processions and the incense, the silver and the vestments? Do they get in the way of how you taught us to be – lowly and quiet and poor – or do they glorify God and make praises ring with the beauty (which I guess is what we had in mind)?"

The eyes of Jesus could make a sphinx look unsophisticated. "I love them," he says. I mull over this statement and conclude it doesn't tell me as much as at first appears. I mean – God loves the entire world, right?

But there's something else I want to know. Something I have always wondered. In our church, there is this woman I once worked for – she manages a small factory in the industrial estate. Not once but twice she did something in her dealings with me that I considered seriously unjust. But I do like to give people the benefit of the doubt. I try to see things from their point of view. And what *was* her point of view? I wondered. What was her motivation? Is she wily and mean? Does she hate me? Is she just indifferent? Not only that, our paths crossed again in later life when I fell into hard times, and I had to go to her for a job. I was desperate, you know? She had vacancies, it would have been easy; but she said no. She had her reasons – which struck me as flimsy – and she wouldn't budge. And when she and I work on projects together at church, the things she says feel like digs, like gibes. And what I want to know is – what is she thinking? Have I got her all wrong? Has she just no clue how bad she makes me feel? Is she doing it on purpose, or have I just got in the way of her armoured car with its poor visibility? Bottom line – is she a complete cow or does she just look that way?

So I ask him. And he listens while I tell him the history and describe the woman. "Yes, I know who you mean," he says.

And then: "I'm sorry to disappoint you," says Jesus. "I think you know what I'm going to say. It's none of your business. What matters – in your life – is what you think, your own motivations. And whether you did your best and meant the kindest. And how you work with the way you feel about her now. And what you say about her. And maybe it also matters to you what I think about you, and about what you did and thought, what you said. We can talk about that if you like. But the rest is between her and me. But – don't you already know that?"

Day 6

Monday of Week 2

Matthew 16:24–27 NIV

Then Jesus said to his disciples, "Whoever wants to be my disciple must deny themselves and take up their cross and follow me. For whoever wants to save their life will lose it, but whoever loses their life for me will find it. What good will it be for someone to gain the whole world, yet forfeit their soul? Or what can anyone give in exchange for their soul? For the Son of Man is going to come in his Father's glory with his angels, and then he will reward each person according to what they have done."

The nearest thing to actual wilderness near where I live is the rough end of the park. It loses itself in a long spit of spectacular woodland that plunges down to a streambed bordered with steep rock-faces clad in harts-tongue ferns. When it's been raining (which it has), spontaneous waterfalls make small cascades here and there. I cup my hands and drink the water, which tastes clean and wild. He drinks too, then lets the tumbling water fill his hands again, and this time splashes it onto his face. He holds his hands out for the waterfall to fill a third time. As it runs over and splashes onto the ground he looks my way with those mesmerizing unfathomable eyes; and with a movement too quick to predict he dashes the water in *my* face. The shock of cold takes my breath away. By the time my wits are sufficiently gathered to take vengeance he's already halfway over the stream, balancing along the narrow fallen tree trunk that lies across it. I set off in hot pursuit, but it takes all my concentration to cross the ghyll without falling in. As I set one foot on terra firma I risk a glance up from the ground, to see him standing waiting, his arms crossed, his eyes laughing.

I hadn't thought of wilderness like this.

We take the narrow path along the hillside, but it's slow going because the way is so muddy, and freezing cold. After a while I suggest we go back to my place for a cup of tea, and he doesn't say no.

"So tell me," I challenge him as we sit in my room, each warming fingers red with cold round a steaming mug of Quick Brew, "what I'm to think about this business of taking up my cross every day to follow you. That I cannot be your disciple unless I give up everything. That the cross is mine as well as yours. I'm a coward, Jesus. It's too much for me. What am I to do?"

He blows on his tea and thinks. Then he says I've got the wrong end of the stick. He thinks some more. Now, I'm not actually taking notes here, okay? Just drinking tea and listening. But the gist of what he tells me goes something like this.

The cross – *his* cross, the real one – belonged to the circumstances of *his* life. What he had to do was accept it and embrace it. He asks me if I understand what "passion" means, which when he explains it, it turns out I do not. Passion, he says, is a bit like "passive", in that it means letting something happen to you – accepting a course of events. "Suffering" apparently means the same – not struggling against what life lands in your lap; embracing it.

The only way for the will of God to be expressed in my life, so that I tune in to God, align myself with God, is to – he flashes me a quick grin – "surrender your agenda"; that's what he says.

He says that my cross won't be the same as his because we're all different; but it will mean turning away from self-interest in the same way. Sometimes it will be huge things that I just can't see how to get through, things that cost everything. Sometimes it'll be small irritations that just catch me on the raw. But that's why it has to be taking up the cross daily – this "surrendering my agenda" and embracing trustfully what life offers me is for every day and never easy.

"So..." I ponder this, "you mean... I never try to change anything? Just go with the flow?"

No, he says; not that. You do the right thing, the appropriate thing, for the circumstances life offers you. But you have to accept the circumstances to get the right thing right. If you use your energy struggling against what is, you lose touch with what the Father is doing. The touching place with God is what is right here right now. And sometimes, it is the cross. That's all. It doesn't mean life's out to get you, to torture you – only, occasionally what has your name on it hurts. And then, struggling against it in angst and complaining and hand-wringing "why me" just makes it worse. To act effectively and appropriately and *gracefully*, you have to start with acceptance; pick up the cross and get on with it.

"Oh," I say. I'm not sure I've understood.

"And about giving up everything –" he continues, but then he looks at my face. "Should we save that for another day? Just the cross for today?"

"No," I say, "keep going."

And he explains that just as the cross means what real life is really offering you, and that if you want to walk the path he walked and follow him you have to learn to stay in touch with what God is doing in the here and now through the circumstances of your life, so you have to learn the art of allowing the things that aren't that to leave you.

"What?" I respond, after thinking about this for some minutes.

"We'll come back to it," he says with a smile. "Nobody gets the hang of this stuff straight away."

And I can't get anything more out of him all afternoon.

Day 7

Tuesday of Week 2

Matthew 13:3, 7, 22 GNT

Once there was a man who went out to sow grain...

... Some of the seed fell among thorn bushes, which grew up and choked the plants.

... The seeds that fell among thorn bushes stand for those who hear the message; but the worries about this life and the love for riches choke the message, and they don't bear fruit.

We make our way down the small path between the houses leading to the park, treading carefully because some dogs have been waiting all night to get into the park and fulfil the call of nature. Not every dog makes it all the way down the path. There are special bins; some dog-owners make use of them diligently. Others don't.

Either side of the path through gaps in close-boarded fencing we catch glimpses of back gardens with their greenhouses, shrubs, and small lawns – all forlorn and straggly still; spring hasn't really got going.

Halfway down the path we come to the end of the gardens and I stop.

"All that there," I say, waving a wide arc to indicate the wasteland covered comprehensively with an overgrowth of brambles, an area of land left to take care of itself between the houses and the park, "is what wilderness means to me. Brambles."

We stand and gaze at the huge briar patch with its impenetrable tangle of thorns. In the woodland of Sussex where I live, brambles are part of the cycle of life determined by light in the coppices. Under the dappling shade of the close-spaced sweet chestnuts chosen for their swift growth and habit of self-renewal after cutting, not much grows – moss, maybe, and fungi. But when a section of trees has been cut, the wild flowers return – bluebells, primroses, and wood anemones in the spring, and wild garlic along the borders of the trees and the banks of streams. As the year progresses the brambles throw out new shoots, long vigorous runners across the bridleways and footpaths, tangling your feet and catching on your clothes. Come the autumn, we go blackberrying; the first fruits of August are the fullest and sweetest, but the main crop comes in September.

Right now the bramble patch is just an ugly tangle of sere grey-brown. It looks dead, but it shelters hidden life, home to rabbits and voles, shrews and field mice, and any number of insects. This is how I think of wilderness.

"Thorns," I say, "thorns that crowd and choke the sprouting seed, leaving no room for anything but themselves. Like that story in the Bible – oh! That was one of your stories, wasn't it?"

"It was," he affirms.

"Well, I think of wilderness like that – both in real life, nature I mean, and as a metaphor. I think one kind of wilderness is the hopelessness that can seize a person, so that nothing can ever get started. I remember you said about the thorns being the cares and the pleasures of this world. So the cares sprout and multiply – money worries and debts, concerns about image and appearance, keeping up with the Joneses, academic and professional success, maybe redundancy and mortgage repossession – a tangling clutter of things that trip you up and catch you fast until you feel as though you'll never be free again, never know again the simplicity you once had in being a child. And the pleasures too – drinking and flirting and sexual voyeurism, shopping till you drop and accumulating possessions; we call it consumerism, but what is consumed? The person's own living soul, in the end.

"Instead of something productive and orderly, a life turns into a wilderness of uncontrolled overgrowth. You can't do anything with it and there's no way through."

Down in the valley where the park nestles, our feet come to rest at the edge of the duck pond, where we crumble the multi-seeded brown rolls I brought, and throw bread to water birds thronging eagerly to be fed on this cold day.

"How about you?" I ask. "If you could pick one thing – like brambles – and say, 'this to me means wilderness', what would it be?"

I watch him, waiting curiously for his response. He looks down at the broken bread he holds, his hands stilled for a moment. Then, he pulls a piece off, crumbling and flinging it across the pond to where less dominant ducks wait their turn. "Stones," he says.

As he says that, suddenly it comes alive in me. I think of subsistence farmers struggling to make something grow in lands where the desert is spreading, and forest dwellers driven off the land by the aggressive encroachment of Western agribusiness, more than a hundred and fifty acres lost every minute of every day, to meet the ever-expanding demands of growth economy, voracity that cannot be satisfied. We have made wilderness our business, leaving nothing but parched and barren scar tissue. We have swapped the people's bread for stones.

Wilderness is two things, then: a beautiful ecosystem teeming with life, and an emptied desert of despair. I suppose a long time ago something happened to our way of looking at things, so that we began to ask only "What's in it for me?" And then the wilderness of the rainforest seemed neither more nor less valuable to us than a ruined barren scar. Somewhere we became destructively utilitarian, and began to dismiss every acre of land not conquered and subjugated as "wilderness".

Yes. Stones, even more than brambles, speak of wilderness.

Day 8

Wednesday of Week 2

Numbers 9:15–17, 20–21 NIV

From evening till morning the cloud above the tabernacle looked like fire. That is how it continued to be; the cloud covered it, and at night it looked like fire. Whenever the cloud lifted from above the tent, the Israelites set out; wherever the cloud settled, the Israelites set up camp… Sometimes the cloud was over the tabernacle for only a few days; at the Lord's command they would set up camp, and then at his command they would set out. Sometimes the cloud stayed only from evening till morning, and when it lifted in the morning, they set out.

1 Kings 8:10–13 NIV

When the priests withdrew from the Holy Place, the cloud filled the temple of the Lord. And the priests could not perform their service because of the cloud, for the glory of the Lord filled his temple. Then Solomon said, "The Lord has said that he would dwell in a dark cloud; I have indeed built a magnificent temple for you, a place for you to dwell for ever."

Job 36:29 NIV

Who can understand how he spreads out the clouds, how he thunders from his pavilion?

Job 35:4–5 NIV

I would like to reply to you and to your friends with you.
Look up at the heavens and see; gaze at the clouds so high
above you.

My room is tiny – 6'8" x 9' to be precise – but it's a kind of Tardis, full of space and peace. This is because I have so little stuff. I have a floor bed that occupies the width of the room under the window, which faces north and overlooks the street. I have a small set of shelves I nailed together from the wood scraps when we took down a garden fence some years ago. I have a large set of shelves made from redundant scaffold boards and gravel boards that occupies the space that isn't filled up by the door in the wall opposite the window. I have a bedside table made of a cardboard box with a big book on top. Everything I own fits comfortably on the shelves, and my coat and hat hang on pegs on the door. An old blanket serves as a curtain strung along the front of the big shelves to keep the busyness of contents from the eye. I have one picture on the wall, above a shelf, of a quiet face with eyes closed in prayer. On the shelf below it is an olive oil lamp made on Mount Sion, the kind Jesus used to have when he lived at home with Mary and Joseph in Nazareth.

I spend a lot of time in this room. It is to me like a monk's cell. It's where I work, think, pray, read, and sleep. During the day, the pillows of the bed range along the wall sofa-style, and a bean bag either end completes it into a comfy nest where friends can sit and chat. That's where we are today, one of us sitting at either end of this bed, under the window. Because it's a floor bed, you can't see the street through the window when you sit here, only the sky.

He has been listening to me complain. I have been mentally wringing my hands about the inexorable spread of concrete across the landscape. Will there be no blade of grass left? Don't they know that trees protect us against both drought and flood? Haven't they understood that trees are the lungs of the earth? Cars and concrete – everywhere! What will become of us? The trees slow down the movement of water through the landscape, so the falling rain settles into the thirsty earth and replenishes the aquifers. The trees shelter us against the heat of the sun and release cooling moisture into the air so we don't need air conditioning. Without trees there is only desert – concrete desert in our case – where the rainfall runs off in flash floods. The earth is dying, drowning and thirsty and choked and poisoned, and we have done this! Outside in the street, apart from the metalled roads and unrelenting rows of ugly shop fronts, the only forest is of poles. Dark wooden telegraph poles with their spiderwebs of telecommunications; metal poles for street name signs, parking signs, traffic signs, waving poles with fluttering advertising flags – and people moan about windfarms being ugly! Where is wildness for us urban dwellers? Where is wilderness for us? It's all gone! Where is freedom and beauty, silence and wide spaces and peace?

He has been quietly contemplating me as I launch this diatribe at him, but as I finally run out of words and sit glaring at him hopelessly, he turns his head towards the window and sits looking at the sky. It is early morning, the household not up for breakfast yet. In the distance you can hear traffic and the sound of the bus engines in the depot along the road. A dog barking. The running feet of an early-rising toddler in the house next door. But mostly in these first hours of the day, the world is still. The sun has risen, but less than an hour ago.

Through the window, I watch what he is watching – the pageant of passing clouds, majestic, slow, freighted with glory. Here and there azure and sapphire peep in ragged triangles through the sublime procession. Great mountainous cumulous ships reflect the newborn sun in golden glory, and their topmost ranges shine resplendent in purest radiance of white. Scudding along below them shredded tissues of violet storm cloud run before the wind. Magnificence. Beauty. Peace. Open and wild, spacious and free. Slow. Pure.

The extravaganza of clouds draws my soul up out of my body, and drenches my thoughts with purity. While earth remains – this gift of beauty.

He says nothing. He just sits quietly, watching the clouds.

Day 9

Thursday of Week 2

John 10:3–4, 7–9 NRSV

The gatekeeper opens the gate for him, and the sheep hear his voice. He calls his own sheep by name and leads them out. When he has brought out all his own, he goes ahead of them, and the sheep follow him because they know his voice... "Very truly, I tell you, I am the gate for the sheep. All who came before me are thieves and bandits; but the sheep did not listen to them. I am the gate. Whoever enters by me will be saved, and will come in and go out and find pasture."

Psalm 127:1–2 RSV

Unless the Lord builds the house, those who build it labour in vain.
Unless the Lord watches over the city, the watchman stays awake in vain.
It is in vain that you rise up early and go late to rest, eating the bread of anxious toil; for he gives to his beloved sleep.

1 Timothy 2:1–2, 8 RSV

First of all, then, I urge that supplications, prayers, intercessions, and thanksgivings be made for all men, for kings and all who are in high positions, that we may lead a quiet and peaceable life, godly and respectful in every way... I desire then that in every place the men should pray, lifting holy hands without anger or quarrelling...

1 Thessalonians 4:1, 11–12 NIV

As for other matters, brothers and sisters, we instructed you how to live in order to please God, as in fact you are living. Now we ask you and urge you in the Lord Jesus to do this more and more… and to make it your ambition to lead a quiet life: you should mind your own business and work with your hands, just as we told you, so that your daily life may win the respect of outsiders and so that you will not be dependent on anybody.

"I read in a leaflet produced by a monastic community that the priory should reflect the peace and order of heaven."

I notice the little grin on Jesus's face as I share this memory with him. "What?" I say. Is there something about heaven that he knows and I don't – well, to be fair I suppose there must be. Or is it what he knows about the priory? "What?" I say again; but he won't be drawn.

So if he's not talking I might as well be.

"Everything is made better by living simply. If I de-clutter my schedule and am really disciplined about what I take on, I am more spacious inside. I get less stressed and I don't resent people. I'm happy to see them. When I have too much to do, everyone's a nuisance and I cross the road when I see them coming."

I pause and think. "How did you do it?" I ask him. "When you had people clamouring for your help night and day – how did you manage to be sitting quietly by the well in Samaria doing nothing in particular when that woman came by? How did you make so much time to pray?"

Jesus considers. "It's about listening," he ventures. "On the inside, always listening for the Father's voice. Watching what he's doing and moving with the flow of that. Like a dance – a dance can be fast, and there are lots of steps, but it isn't busy or chaotic; you just follow the music."

I like that idea – a dance instead of a timetable.

"It's the same with possessions," I add. "The less you have, the less there is to organize and clean and trip over. Your house gets bigger if there's not much in it. So you don't need to upgrade to a massive mortgage just to have somewhere to stash all your junk – 'cause there isn't any."

Why am I saying this to Jesus? What can I possibly have to tell him about simplicity? But he nods in agreement. "It's easier to concentrate on the people," he says, "when you aren't always worrying about the things. Stuff you can't see as well – invisible trophies like status and achievements, being important and well-thought of, being right. It's all mental furniture. And, you can't really be alongside people if they're envious of what you have or what you are, if you have what they always wanted and it's eating them up inside. It makes it harder to be their friend. If you just have nothing, it's easier for them to concentrate on what you say and how you live – because what else is there? Easier for you to concentrate on it, for the same reason."

"And no arguing!" I chime in. "No wars and no career ladders, no stepping over other people to reach the top."

A quiet life… the peace and order of heaven… learning the steps of the dance that goes with the music of life… being as free to come and go as a sheep is free to follow the shepherd out to pasture and safe home to the fold – no briefcase to carry, no image to keep up; just walking along the track with the others, listening for his voice.

"It's such a beautiful way to live," I comment. "So pure in heart, and so free."

"Yeah," says Jesus looking at me sideways, laughing. "And so hard to do! It takes a bit of practice. You haven't to be disheartened if it doesn't come together all at once."

Day 10

Friday of Week 2

Mark 8:31–38 NIV

He then began to teach them that the Son of Man must suffer many things and be rejected by the elders, the chief priests and the teachers of the law, and that he must be killed and after three days rise again. He spoke plainly about this, and Peter took him aside and began to rebuke him.

But when Jesus turned and looked at his disciples, he rebuked Peter. "Get behind me, Satan!" he said. "You do not have in mind the concerns of God, but merely human concerns."

Then he called the crowd to him along with his disciples and said: "Whoever wants to be my disciple must deny themselves and take up their cross and follow me. For whoever wants to save their life will lose it, but whoever loses their life for me and for the gospel will save it. What good is it for someone to gain the whole world, yet forfeit their soul? Or what can anyone give in exchange for their soul? If anyone is ashamed of me and my words in this adulterous and sinful generation, the Son of Man will be ashamed of them when he comes in his Father's glory with the holy angels."

I've been badgering him to tell me more about this giving up everything. What does it mean? Is it like radical communism or voluntary homelessness? Will I still be able to have earrings and follow Jesus? Have I had my last cappuccino at Starbucks or is there hope? "Whoa," he says. "Slow down!"

We're sitting on the beach in the lee of the groyne tattered with bright green weed, sheltering from the wind. I've been hurling pebbles in agitation towards the sea, but I stop now and turn towards him. I need to know about this. I have to understand what is real, what was meant, what is possible.

For a while, as I watch him, he just sits looking out across the ocean, gazing at the heaving grey-green waves and the line of light that rims the far horizon. Something in his stillness carries over to me. As I look at him, I notice my tension and anxiety, and my breath sighs out of me, letting it go. For a moment I feel the wind against my face, so keen and alive, feel the curve of my body huddled there, feel the life in my hands, my feet, all of me. I come back from my turmoiling questions to just be here, as he is here, apparently at peace.

And then he begins to explain it to me.

He says, we are made in the image of God, and God is I Am That I Am. Present Presence. He says God is not defined by anything or identified with anything – he just is – and in this totality of being he creates. Do I understand? "No," I say. He smiles.

Well, he says, we have this way of losing ourselves in what we desire. Like, if I am thin I will be beautiful and if I am beautiful I will be attractive, and if I am attractive I will be loved. Or maybe we want to be clever and admired, so instead of listening in a conversation we sit thinking up smart things to say, just waiting our turn to prove our intelligence. Or else we think if we can have a bigger house, a more modern car, a faster computer, life will be so much better. We go into debt running after the things that will make us happy – and then conclude that what will make us happy now is more money.

And all the time, we are trying to put together a life from what's out there, overlooking completely that life is *in here*, inside. We are already made in the image of God. In leaving that to go out of ourselves after things we hope will validate us and give us worth and substance and kudos, we lose touch with the essential vitality of being which we have been given as our birthright.

By chasing after life out there, we run away from life in here. But life isn't out there; it's in here or nowhere at all.

Once you know that, once you really see that you are made in the image of God, I Am That I Am, all that stuff out there loses its hold on you. You wake up to the realization that everything you wanted – love, happiness, freedom, truth, peace – is inside not outside. It is already given; you just have to take hold of it and unpack it and act on it.

"The thing is," he says, turning his head to look at me, "giving up everything sounds like a terrible loss. I know it does. But hanging on to it all is like clutching the chocolate wrapper and throwing away the chocolate. The sweetness of life is not outside you, whether in possessions or the good opinion of others or being right or being clever or beautiful or rich. Going after those is only chasing the wind. But the tragedy is not in the waste of time, it's in what you could have had instead; the richness and wonder of being who you really are – a reflection of God."

I think about this. It sounds too good to be true.

"So… it's not hard then, this giving up everything?" I can't keep the incredulity out of my voice.

"It's hard if you try to force it," he says, picking a pebble up and cupping it gently in his hand. "But as soon as you see things for what they are, it's just… obvious."

Day 11

Saturday of Week 2

Luke 3:15–17 NIV

*The people were waiting expectantly and were all wondering
in their hearts if John might possibly be the Messiah. John
answered them all, "I baptise you with water. But one who is
more powerful than I will come, the straps of whose sandals
I am not worthy to untie. He will baptise you with the Holy
Spirit and fire. His winnowing fork is in his hand to clear his
threshing-floor and to gather the wheat into his barn, but he will
burn up the chaff with unquenchable fire."*

Luke 12:49 NIV

*"I have come to bring fire on the earth, and how I wish it were
already kindled!"*

John 21:7–12 NIV

*Then the disciple whom Jesus loved said to Peter, "It is the
Lord!" As soon as Simon Peter heard him say, "It is the Lord,"
he wrapped his outer garment round him (for he had taken it
off) and jumped into the water. The other disciples followed in
the boat, towing the net full of fish, for they were not far from
shore, about a hundred metres. When they landed, they saw a
fire of burning coals there with fish on it, and some bread.*

*Jesus said to them, "Bring some of the fish you have just
caught." So Simon Peter climbed back into the boat and dragged the*

net ashore. It was full of large fish, 153, but even with so many the net was not torn. Jesus said to them, "Come and have breakfast."

None of the disciples dared ask him, "Who are you?" They knew it was the Lord.

So, I have everything stacked perfectly in the woodstove – at either end, upright in the bed of last night's ashes, I've stood a solid hardwood log. Two sentinels, stalwart, they guard the mound in the middle, scrunched paper under a wigwam of short kindling slats, softwood mainly. Then across the top, longer kindling slats balanced from log to log with two chunky bits of short split wood topping it all off, ready to fall through burning into the middle and become the basis of the fire once the paper and kindling's all gone. What could possibly go wrong?

Only it won't light. Three matches later and I am starting to feel embarrassed. The wood is dry, the paper is the kind that catches well, I've stacked it carefully – what's the problem?

"I think," he ventures humbly, "you might have packed it too tight."

On the subject of fires, I do have to respect his observations. Thirty days and nights in the wilderness must have honed a few skills in igniting damp wood. And I've read the story of his disciples coming in at first light after a night's (fruitless) fishing to find him with a cook-fire going in readiness on the shore. Anyone who can build a successful campfire despite a stiff sea breeze, in a resurrection body that can also walk through walls, has surely got it sussed. So I bow to his superior knowledge, increasing the aperture at the front of my wood wigwam, moving that nice little piece of kindling to a place where the first flames will reach it, because it's good and dry, half burnt now, and should take easily.

This time, I succeed. As it's pouring with rain outside, we spend the morning fire-watching through the window of the woodstove. Wilderness viewing.

It takes a while to get that fire just right. At one point, the material forming the central starter has burnt low, so I add another good big log end-on in the middle, but it and the sentinels are no more than glowing, and the chunky bits I balanced on top haven't fallen through as I'd hoped but stayed balanced, teetering on the edge of the sentinel tops. He suggests I might knock them down with the poker to fill the gaps between the sentinels and the middle log. I do this. Once there is that contact, the fire finally takes hold and we can relax.

"Fires," he observes, "are all about bridges and spaces. If you want a fire to catch, you need both. Things have to be so set up that there's something in place as a bridge to carry the flame from one to the next, but leaving spaces so the fire can breathe and the flame is not suffocated."

I know him well enough by this time to grasp that he is, and is not, discussing wood, flame, and newspaper. He means people. He means Holy Spirit. He means souls. This is the man who came to set the whole world ablaze. He knows how to start a fire. Time in the press and throng of the community, teaching, healing, listening, loving. And time up in the hills, out in the wilderness, alone with God.

Sitting silently, watching the flames move along the logs now touching, I think of the bridge he made, the crossing place. The wood they nailed him to, that joined up heaven and earth, that let the fire of love travel through to ignite such a blaze as two thousand years has not extinguished. It exposed a world choked with sin to the oxygen of heaven, that bridge of rough wood. They hammered in the nails through his wrists and his feet while the cross lay still in the dust of the earth. Then they hoisted it high, its foot in a socket of earth and the top of it in heaven, crossing the gap, with him nailed to the wood. No other way could the firebreak be bridged. "I'll go. I'll do it." Yes, he knows about fire.

Day 12

Second Sunday in Lent

Luke 6:37–42 NIV

"Do not judge, and you will not be judged. Do not condemn, and you will not be condemned. Forgive, and you will be forgiven. Give, and it will be given to you. A good measure, pressed down, shaken together and running over, will be poured into your lap. For with the measure you use, it will be measured to you."

He also told them this parable: "Can the blind lead the blind? Will they not both fall into a pit? The student is not above the teacher, but everyone who is fully trained will be like their teacher.

"Why do you look at the speck of sawdust in your brother's eye and pay no attention to the plank in your own eye? How can you say to your brother, 'Brother, let me take the speck out of your eye,' when you yourself fail to see the plank in your own eye? You hypocrite, first take the plank out of your eye, and then you will see clearly to remove the speck from your brother's eye."

Luke 18:9–14 RSV

He also told this parable to some who trusted in themselves that they were righteous and despised others: "Two men went up into the temple to pray, one a Pharisee and the other a tax collector. The Pharisee stood and prayed thus with himself, 'God, I thank thee that I am not like other men, extortioners, unjust, adulterers, or even like this tax collector. I fast twice a week, I give tithes of all that I get.' But the tax collector, standing far off, would not even lift up his eyes to heaven, but beat his breast, saying, 'God, be merciful to

*me a sinner!' I tell you, this man went down to his house justified
rather than the other; for every one who exalts himself will be
humbled, but he who humbles himself will be exalted."*

I don't know what your Facebook page is like but mine is plastered
with petitions to sign and links to articles about veganism, justice
and peace initiatives, simple living stories, groovy permaculturist
gardening ventures, and sustainable building projects. I have
among my friends Anglicans, Baptists, Community Church
members, Quakers, Buddhists, Eastern and Greek Orthodox,
Atheists, Methodists, Catholics, and a few more besides. So most
days on Facebook also bring a smattering of postings with Bible
verses, links to articles about faith and practice, and inspirational
posters with edifying texts superimposed on beautiful pictures.

Jesus is very interested in Facebook. He likes to read what
friends are saying to each other, and look at the patterns of what
they care about revealed in their posts. He comments very little,
but he reads thoughtfully and thoroughly, sitting cross-legged on
my bed looking at the laptop.

"What?" I ask, as he shakes his head with a smile expressing
what I can best describe as resigned amusement. "What's up?"

"They don't get my joke," he says. "They never get that
joke, and it was a good one."

He wriggles along so I can sit beside him and look where he
is pointing on my timeline. A Lenten post from a friend in the
States: "Brothers and sisters we must not be like that Pharisee
when we pray! For whoever exalts himself must be abased. Let
us humble ourselves by fasting so our prayers will be acceptable
to God."

I look at the post. I look at Jesus. "What joke?"

There's not a lot of space for two people at the end of my
bed, so I leave him at his end with the laptop and go back to my
nest at the further end. "Jesus? What joke?"

I can't quite get used to the eyes of Jesus. I will always remember them. Brimming with life and laughter, with intelligence and wisdom, really seeing me, challenging, holding nothing back.

"It's not so funny if you have to explain it," he says.

"Even so?" I wait for him to tell me.

"My story about the Pharisee and the tax collector," he explains. "The point is it's only half a story. The first half is the bit I tell, where the Pharisee looks at the tax collector and shudders and thinks, 'I'm glad I'm not like him!'

"But that's not the end of the story. The next part happens off the page, in the life of the person reading, who looks at the Pharisee and thinks, 'I'm glad I'm not like him!'

"Not hilarious, I know, but the joke was that you can't help doing it. You can't get away from it – judgments and assumptions, opinions and evaluations; and then put-downs and condemnations, ostracizing and dismissing. The whole world is full of people looking at each other and thinking, 'I'm glad I'm not like him.'

"It wasn't meant to be an anti-Pharisee dig. They were okay, the Pharisees – well, some of them were. It was meant to be a reminder, a trigger, something that would linger in the memory to help you catch yourself doing it and break the habit.

"But people hear it and nod sagely, and think how awful Pharisees are, and start looking round for Pharisees to identify and write off."

"Oh," I say. "Oh, right." I hadn't realized.

Jesus shrugs. "I don't mind them not getting the joke. But it's disappointing if it's seen as permission to isolate yet another group to vilify and point the finger at. The bottom line is, if you think you're not like them, you are. Because we're all in this together."

Day 13

Monday of Week 3

John 9:26–30 NIV

Then they asked him, "What did he do to you? How did he open your eyes?"

He answered, "I have told you already and you did not listen. Why do you want to hear it again? Do you want to become his disciples too?"

Then they hurled insults at him and said, "You are this fellow's disciple! We are disciples of Moses! We know that God spoke to Moses, but as for this fellow, we don't even know where he comes from."

The man answered, "Now that is remarkable! You don't know where he comes from, yet he opened my eyes."

John 3:1–3 NIV

Now there was a Pharisee, a man named Nicodemus who was a member of the Jewish ruling council. He came to Jesus at night and said, "Rabbi, we know that you are a teacher who has come from God. For no one could perform the signs you are doing if God were not with him."

Jesus replied, "Very truly I tell you, no one can see the kingdom of God unless they are born again."

Romans 12:2 NIV

Do not conform to the pattern of this world, but be transformed by the renewing of your mind. Then you will be able to test and approve what God's will is – his good, pleasing and perfect will.

"What you see," he remarks, "is what you get."

I smile, nodding, glancing across to catch his eye.

"Absolutely," I affirm. "No games. No hidden agendas. Mmhmm."

We continue to stroll along the muddy path alongside the stream. Mist hangs about the old trees and dark green rhododendrons bordering the path. Every now and then some bird flits across in front of us, hoping to attract our attention in case we have bread. We don't. I forgot to bring any.

"Well," he says, "that's true. But I didn't mean just the way things are with me. I meant, in the whole of life what you see is what you get."

I wrinkle my nose, puzzled. "I don't think so," I venture after a while. "There's the advertising industry for a start, where what you see is one thing and what you get is anybody's guess, Advertising Standards Agency or not. And people are forever trying to manipulate each other, pulling strings and pressing buttons, working a situation to their own advantage, making themselves look good and the other person look stupid or at fault. In my world, what-you-see-is-what-you-get is a treasure, a one in a million find."

"Even so," he persists, "the world – your world – and everything in it, will not be the same as the world someone else lives in. You think you both live in the same world, but you don't. Because what you see is what you get."

"Go on," I say resignedly, "explain."

He has a way of flashing a sideways glance at me, questioning, challenging. "I am listening," I promise.

"Remember that homeless man we saw begging when we walked through the town last week?"

I nod in affirmation. "Yep."

"Some people passing him think, 'There but for the grace of God go I', and toss him a coin as they wonder momentarily what went wrong in his life, how he got himself into that situation. Some people drop money onto his jacket spread out there and it triggers rage in them that our society messes people's lives up like this, that government corruption and welfare benefit cuts and mismanaged economies could have destroyed a man's life, reduced a citizen to begging on the streets. And some people feel a surge of righteous indignation because nobody gave them a hand up – nobody ever gave them anything – they worked to be where they are now and earned every penny of what they have, and if that man wants a slice of it he should get up off the floor and do the same. It's just one man sitting in the subway begging for loose change, but it might as well be three different ones. The world you live in depends entirely on how you see it. You stopped and exclaimed in delight at the sweet little squirrel that ran along the tree limb to greet us just now. Some people just think they're vermin. How you see things depends on your preconceptions. That's why you have to be born again to see the kingdom of God.

"You have to give up your way of seeing things, and realize that your vision is smudged and blurry. You have birdlime on your windscreen, and when you switch on the wipers they just spread it around. You can't see properly. You need to let me wash it off for you, clear it all away. Preconceptions. Birdlime. The way you look at things. If you let me renew your mind, if you let the inside you be reborn and start again, you'll see things the way I do – differently."

He stops for a moment and stands quite still. A small brown bird has landed on a twig barely a yard away. I watch his face, so kind, so full of love. Bright-eyed, the bird cocks its head and looks right back at him, then speaks a little trill before hopping nonchalantly away along the branch.

"The thing is," he continues as we set off walking again, "the kingdom of God is there all the time. It's all around. It's arrived.

But you can say that to people until you're blue in the face and they still don't get it. Because they can't see it, and the reason they can't see it is their preconceptions are interfering with their vision. They think seeing is believing, think they believe what they do because of the way the world is, when all along it's been the other way around. What you see is what you get."

Day 14

Tuesday of Week 3

Isaiah 43:1–3 NIV

But now, this is what the Lord says –
he who created you, Jacob,
he who formed you, Israel:
"Do not fear, for I have redeemed you;
I have summoned you by name; you are mine.
When you pass through the waters,
I will be with you;
and when you pass through the rivers,
they will not sweep over you.
When you walk through the fire,
you will not be burned;
the flames will not set you ablaze.
For I am the Lord your God,
the Holy One of Israel, your Saviour."

It gets too cold down on the beach, even crouching in the shelter afforded by the corner where the groyne meets the seawall. The sky is wild, more purple than grey, a burgeoning overmass of angry clouds. Seagulls flashing and tossing white against that great spreading bruise of threatening weather. Eventually I've had enough and we head off home to light a fire. Halfway up the hill, the downpour starts.

Before five minutes pass, rain is splashing and gurgling, streams are forming in the gutters, my glasses are all steamed up, my hair is plastered to my head, rain is even dripping down my neck, I am freezing and shivering.

All around, people are darting and jostling, impatient to get out of the wet, taking risks crossing the road, getting in each other's way, having a hard time seeing anything as they hurry with shoulders hunched and heads bent, irritable and swearing.

It's a long way up the hill. I start to feel really, really sorry for myself. My feet are actually squelching in my shoes. I do have enough money for a bus ride as it happens, but only for me – and there's no point asking Jesus; if there's one thing I've learned by now it's that he *never* has any money. Nothing for it but to pull my coat a bit tighter and keep plodding, then. I hate the cold. I hate the rain. I hate the wind. I wish the sun would shine. I long for the summer. I'm sick of darkness and horrible weather. I wish this would just stop.

I feel him tap my arm, and squint sideways at him through the downpour. He's grinning at me (why?), his hair stuck to his face in wet rivulets, rain on his eyelashes, his face one whole river of rain.

And he's holding out his hand to me, the rain running over it and dripping up his sleeve.

I take his hand.

The difference comes as a shock – like a real shock I mean, like an electric shock. Something powerful. For one thing, it's as though joy courses into my body, my whole being, flowing in until I am saturated with this effervescent joy that fills me until I feel like it could spout out of the top of my head like a whale blowing. But as well as that, it just boggles my mind to think that here I am – ordinary me – walking down this street – this ordinary street – holding hands with Jesus. I have to tell it to myself; I'm holding hands with Jesus, and say it a second time because I can hardly take it in.

Without my noticing it, my whole body has relaxed. He is

walking slowly, and because we're holding hands I have to go slower too, and I can't grip on to my coat either. I have to do what he's doing – walk through rain as if it was sunshine, slowly and joyfully, letting it be cold, letting it be wet. He is holding my hand – what does it matter if it's raining?

I've stopped hurrying, stopped hunching and squinting. It's as though I'm breathing for the first time, expanding like a butterfly newly hatched from a chrysalis, unfolding cramped and crinkled wings into the sunlight.

I treasure every minute of that walk home through the storm. From that moment nothing matters because Jesus is holding my hand.

This is, you understand, an experience not easily forgotten – although I admit I do forget it sometimes.

As I look back on it, I realize that in all the pictures I've seen of Jesus in the wilderness, it's never raining. There are usually rocks and small plants, and Jesus standing looking mystical – or staring hard at a large pebble willing it to be bread. A wilderness of pouring rain, surrounded by shoving pedestrians and passing cars drenching you with puddle spray, with Jesus standing there grinning, his eyes laughing, holding out his hand to you – you wouldn't paint wilderness like that, would you? To be fair, nor would I.

But I know that ever since that day – like a clear before and after – whenever things get unbearable, when I'm cold and wet and miserable and harassed and wish I was anywhere but here – I take a moment, just one moment, to close my eyes and remember him. Standing in the rain, holding out his hand to me.

When I look back on this day, I know I will remember it not so much as the day we got caught by the rain as the day I held hands with Jesus.

All kinds of storms hit and shake me, walking through my own particular stretches of wilderness. I'm trying to learn the trick of not hunching my shoulders, not hurrying through to get out of it as fast as I can. If I stop and think about it, I will remember the feeling of his hand in mine, and find it for myself once again – walking with Jesus though the storm, his hand holding mine, and the joy coursing through. All the way home.

Day 15

Wednesday of Week 3

Luke 10:25–29 NIV

*On one occasion an expert in the law stood up to test Jesus.
"Teacher," he asked, "what must I do to inherit eternal life?"*

*"What is written in the Law?" he replied. "How do you
read it?"*

*He answered, "'Love the Lord your God with all your heart
and with all your soul and with all your strength and with all your
mind'; and, 'Love your neighbour as yourself.'"*

*"You have answered correctly," Jesus replied. "Do this and
you will live."*

*But he wanted to justify himself, so he asked Jesus, "And who
is my neighbour?"*

We hang out the washing together. I've been waiting ages for the
weather to brighten up. The wind these last weeks has brought
squall after squall off the sea, with rain spattering against the
window panes until I've been sick of hearing it. But at last the
clouds have cleared enough to let the sunshine through, and
this day the air shines gloriously clean, the wind still blowing;
obviously my cue to get on with the family's laundry, which has
been stacking up waiting.

Now, I have a method when I peg up the clothes, and
glancing over I'm not at all sure that he has, but hey – they're
flapping in the breeze and he's helping. That's okay, isn't it?

Doing chores together is an excellent way to get to know someone. It can be easier to chat while you're both engaged in a task, and the silences that arrive are easy and natural, without anyone needing to fill them for the sake of politeness like you do at a party. Plus somehow, when I'm busy, it wakes up my mind, and all kinds of thoughts come bustling in I didn't even know were waiting at the door.

"My neighbour" (this is one of the thoughts that has evidently been waiting out in the cold): "how can I tell who is my neighbour?

"I mean, every time I turn on the computer I'm bombarded with all these images. The day before yesterday a photo of a child stopped me in my tracks. She was squatting by a dusty road, with her head dropped in her hands; thin, naked, enveloped in despair. The advert offered me the chance to help 'a child like her' – implying there are millions! But I wanted to help *her* – actually *her* – even though I only have twenty pounds in my current account. I wanted to pick her up and bring her home. But I can't, can I? My heart tells me she is my neighbour, but common sense and my knowledge of geography tell me she's as unreachable as the moon. Setting up another monthly direct debit to a missionary organization doesn't feel a bit like helping my neighbour. What d'you think? What should I have done?

"And there was another child, a poor scrap of a thing in a cot in some institution in Eastern Europe. 'Thousands like these waiting for adoption,' the article said. Adoption? I don't think so, not at my age!

"But that was only the beginning of it. After that came the picture of a sad dog and a caption urging me to offer a home to a gentle greyhound, and one reminding me how little it costs to save the sight of someone in Africa or India who without my help will be completely blind. And the pictures of refugees emerging barefoot along the track through clouds of blowing dust, gaunt and tired, carrying their worldly goods in cloth bundles on their heads.

"All of them, apparently, need my help. I don't know where to start. I can't see how to begin.

"And then I met Elaine on the bus and she'd been so poorly. She's nearly ninety now, and she feels so vulnerable at times. She had bronchitis and phoned the emergency doctor because she felt so ill it scared her. Guess what they told her? Go to the hospital and see the emergency doctor there. So she had a fifteen-minute walk to the bus stop, a twenty-minute wait for the hospital bus, and a forty-five-minute wait in the hospital waiting room. By then it was late and she still had to get back home. Elaine needs a neighbour. And I heard Raymond has gone into a home now, because his macular degeneration has got so bad there's nothing right in front of him but a blank space. He could really do with a visitor right now. And then last night a woman passing in the street screamed at her kids so loudly it made me wince. But I know that woman. She looks so tired sometimes. She hardly ever gets out. And I think it's been hard to make the money stretch since her husband left – and I know she's frightened of losing the house if they can't keep up the payments.

"So many people who need so much. So little of me. Which one do I pick? Where do I begin?"

I've stopped what I was doing, and stand waving my hands in the air helplessly, illustrating point after point with wild and impotent gestures.

He doesn't reply.

He doesn't look at me.

He just gets on with the job.

One item of laundry at a time, in no particular order, just as they present themselves on the pile; he picks them up, shakes them out, and hangs them in the sunshine and fresh air.

What seemed like a European Washing Mountain now

blows gaily in the breeze, firmly anchored by pegs that he's picked up from the basket one by one.

Later that day, before the evening damps, I come out into the garden again, take it all down, fold it up and bring it indoors. Next week there'll be the same load to do all over again, and the week after that. The ordinary rhythm of service, the mundane tasks of responsibility – the unexceptional face of love.

Week by week, day by day, one by one.

Day 16

Thursday of Week 3

Matthew 7:1–5 GNT

"Do not judge others, so that God will not judge you, for God will judge you in the same way you judge others, and he will apply to you the same rules you apply to others. Why, then, do you look at the speck in your brother's eye and pay no attention to the log in your own eye? How dare you say to your brother, 'Please, let me take that speck out of your eye,' when you have a log in your own eye? You hypocrite! First take the log out of your own eye, and then you will be able to see clearly to take the speck out of your brother's eye."

James 3:13–18 GNT

Are there any of you who are wise and understanding? You are to prove it by your good life, by your good deeds performed with humility and wisdom. But if in your heart you are jealous, bitter, and selfish, don't sin against the truth by boasting of your wisdom. Such wisdom does not come down from heaven; it belongs to the world, it is unspiritual and demonic. Where there is jealousy and selfishness, there is also disorder and every kind of evil. But the wisdom from above is pure first of all; it is also peaceful, gentle, and friendly; it is full of compassion and produces a harvest of good deeds; it is free from prejudice and hypocrisy. And goodness is the harvest that is produced from the seeds the peacemakers plant in peace.

I went to Quaker meeting, and enjoyed the silence for a while, until somebody said something that really annoyed me: "It says in the Bible, 'As you think, so shall you become.'" I can't remember the rest of what they said, because that irritated me so much I stopped listening.

Walking home through the park, I see Jesus. The sight of him, strolling peacefully, looking at the birds as he goes, and the new shoots of plants showing through last year's leaf-mould, restores my happiness. When I catch up with him, I tell him about the Quaker ministry that got on my nerves. "They said that it says in the Bible, 'As you think so shall you become'! Can you believe it?"

"Oh, certainly." He nods in affirmation. "It's absolutely true."

I gaze at him, incredulous. This is Jesus, right? "It may be true," I say, "but it isn't in the Bible. Bruce Lee said it."

"That's okay, isn't it?" He looks at me, questioning. "Bruce Lee wasn't born when they decided what would go in the Bible."

"No, it's not okay – it's incorrect. It's really important to stick to the facts with the Bible. Otherwise you end up with people saying, 'As the prophet said – I have a dream...' or 'In the words of the psalmist, Go placidly amid the noise and haste, and remember what peace there may be in silence.'"

Again, Jesus only nods. I look at him sharply. He does *know*? "The first one is Martin Luther King, Jr and the second one's Max Ehrmann," I say, hoping this may be unnecessary.

"Everyone needs a dream," he says, "and there is great peace in the silence."

This conversation is not going the way I'd imagined.

"Doesn't it matter?" I challenge him, exasperated. "You think it's okay to misquote the Scriptures and lead people down false trails about what is and isn't in the Bible?"

"Life rooted in the Scriptures is strong and secure," he says. "But the important thing really is to live it – I mean, that's what it's for. The Scriptures weren't written to make people right; they're seeds of grace to make life beautiful."

We walk along a bit further, and Jesus talks quietly – and sadly, I think – about the acrimony of church splits and depth of its divisions; about the vitriol with which the faithful denounce sins they use the Bible to identify and condemn in the life of others. He speaks about the need people feel to define themselves by fighting an opposition, strengthening their identity by conflict with a supposed enemy, identifying with their own stance and position, losing sight of everything except their grim hold on the insistence that they are right.

"It doesn't matter," he says. "It doesn't matter if they are right. What the Father cares about is if they are kind, if they are loving – if they're willing to overlook mistakes and give the benefit of the doubt. It's a way of living."

"So you are saying –" (my voice sounds confrontational; someone seems to have turned up the volume) "that just anything will do? That what's in the Bible simply doesn't matter?"

Just with his fingertip Jesus touches the back of my hand.

"I'm saying it matters immensely," he replies, "and that what is written is 'Judge not and you shall not be judged, condemn not and you shall not be condemned… love covers a multitude of sins… all of us often make mistakes… we are not fighting against human beings but against the wicked spiritual forces in the heavenly world… love does not keep a record of wrongs.' The wisdom of the Scripture is beautiful with the flexible strength of kindness. Insistence on being right, and the arguments that go with it, make communities brittle."

I digest these words in silence as the path takes us up the hill. I'm not quite ready to let this go. "Jesus," I say, "it really matters to me to know the Scriptures – to search them and learn them and understand their meaning. I cannot believe we can just shrug that off."

"Are you listening to me?" He doesn't sound cross; his voice is peaceable, gentle. "It's about living, not winning."

And I see that if I stick to applying what I read in my own life, without getting antsy about what other people are doing, the problem pretty much just goes away.

Friday of Week 3

Luke 18:17 KJV

Verily I say unto you, Whosoever shall not receive the kingdom of God as a little child shall in no wise enter therein.

Matthew 13:14–17 GNT

"So the prophecy of Isaiah applies to them:

'This people will listen and listen, but not understand;
they will look and look, but not see, because their minds are dull,
and they have stopped up their ears and have closed their eyes.
Otherwise, their eyes would see, their ears would hear, their minds
would understand, and they would turn to me, says God, and I
would heal them.'

"As for you, how fortunate you are! Your eyes see and your ears
hear. I assure you that many prophets and many of God's people
wanted very much to see what you see, but they could not, and to
hear what you hear, but they did not."

We sit side by side, on the floor, watching the flames take hold.

This time I've got the fire alight easily, first time – I did it right.

The twigs spurt into flame from the fire creeping up the side of the cardboard kindled from the crumpled newspaper underneath. The rough edges of the birch logs ignite, and the dried moss catches, then the bark where it grew. It's burning well.

"Did you want a cup of coffee?" I ask. He smiles, and shakes his head. No. Okay.

I ask him if he wants anything to eat, if he'd like me to put the TV on, if there's anything he wants to do.

"Watching the fire is good," he says. "I like watching the fire."

So we sit there, and the minutes go by.

I don't know anyone else whose silence is as comfortable as this. I didn't know I was carrying tension until I feel myself gradually relaxing. I'm the kind of person who looks ahead to the next chore waiting for me, and most of the time in the back of my mind there's a niggling sense of guilt about someone neglected, something unfinished, an approaching deadline, a project incomplete – or, even worse, unstarted. But if Jesus has come to be your guest, you don't need to do anything, do you? Just being with him is enough, is the right thing to be doing.

Sitting there quietly, an odd thing begins to happen. I start to get back something I knew I'd lost but couldn't figure out how to retrieve – the way I used to look at things when I was a child.

In childhood, I used to look at things so carefully, intently. I'd gaze with complete absorption at the minute red spider mites gliding along the flagstones in the sun, or at ants bearing their loads back home. I'd bury my hands in peat compost heaped in preparation for gardening work, and rejoice in the texture of it. I'd chew grass to really live the taste, and lick my knees, which tasted different from my hands. If I found an object and couldn't determine its substance, I'd touch my lips and then my tongue to it – because I knew the tongue-touch of glass, metal, plastic – I knew the feeling of things through intimate association.

Somewhere along the way I stopped really looking, feeling, tasting, knowing. Doing supplanted experiencing. Doing slipped without my realizing into accomplishing. The otherness of anything became a nuisance; I came to view everything as a task.

This is the first time in years I have escaped my world of

teeming obligations and expectations, to do nothing, think nothing, only gaze into the fire.

I suppose in the wilderness lighting a fire is very important – for warmth, for cooking, against insects, for keeping wild animals away. In the wilderness, apart from constructing shelter the main focus of the day must surely be sourcing and preparing food – hunting, gathering, skinning, gutting, wrapping meat in leaves into parcels skewered by wet twigs, all that kind of thing. So if you are *fasting* in the wilderness, for forty days and forty nights, then you fast from occupation as well as from consumption. You are thrown back onto the waiting still emptiness of your own self, to simply be who you are. The fire becomes occupation, companion, expression, involvement…

Sitting at his side, feeling his stillness, the absolute peace about him as he gazes into the flames without speaking, for a moment it is as though we could have been anywhere. For all its containment in the pseudo-Victorian grate, this fire is a moment of wilderness. For the first time in far too long I know I am really seeing, really being – and nothing else.

We sit there like this for ages. I get bored, I get tired, I wonder what to make for tea, I wonder what he's thinking, whether to suggest a walk. I think I might be cold (no, I'm not). And in-between all these wonderings I come back again and again to the living being of the fire, the beauty of flame and ash, the mystery of heat. I see how it is like a dragon, its curling tongues licking at the next piece of wood, how it has to breathe, has to be fed. The fire is a creature, a *person*!

As Jesus leans forward to place fresh wood when the first is consumed, I see how beautiful are his hands and his face in the firelight, see the texture of his homespun wool robe and the locks of his hair.

There is more than one way to see. Most of the time I see pragmatically – assessing, categorizing, evaluating, registering information for future use. But this seeing is how I saw in childhood, a union with the other, a leaving of myself to become all sensory awareness immersed in what I saw. I remember that Jesus taught a lot about learning to see.

Every fire I light from this day on will be my escape into wilderness.

Day 18

Saturday of Week 3

Psalm 19:1–5 NIV

The heavens declare the glory of God;
the skies proclaim the work of his hands.
Day after day they pour forth speech;
night after night they reveal knowledge.
They have no speech, they use no words;
no sound is heard from them.
Yet their voice goes out into all the earth,
their words to the ends of the world.
In the heavens God has pitched a tent for the sun.
It is like a bridegroom coming out of his chamber,
like a champion rejoicing to run his course.

Job 37:4–12 NIV

When his voice resounds,
he holds nothing back.
God's voice thunders in marvellous ways;
he does great things beyond our understanding.
He says to the snow, "Fall on the earth,"
and to the rain shower, "Be a mighty downpour."
So that everyone he has made may know his work,
he stops all people from their labour.
The animals take cover;
they remain in their dens.

The tempest comes out from its chamber,
the cold from the driving winds.
The breath of God produces ice,
and the broad waters become frozen.
He loads the clouds with moisture;
he scatters his lightning through them.
At his direction they swirl around
over the face of the whole earth
to do whatever he commands them.

I wake up early but I (usually) get up late. You know – answering emails, checking out what the world is doing on Facebook, looking to see if there's any money in my current account – all that kind of thing.

This morning I prop myself up on four pillows while the day is still half-dark, foggy and cold. All cosy under my duvet and two blankets, wearing a fleece over my PJs for good measure, I have my laptop propped open against my knees.

Last night on TV I watched this fab film about wilderness survival techniques – how to spear fish with a penknife bound to a long stick with a length of twine, how to chisel out your own canoe from a tree trunk, and making a shelter from scratch with three branches and some bracken.

This morning, inspired, I've been reading the blog of a man who spends his entire time sailing around on a small boat with his wife and two children. Amazing. Now I'm catching up on a film I've meant to get round to watching for ages, about a herbalist who wanders in the hills with her dogs, foraging for medicinal plants which have kept her and everyone she knows in tip-top condition for decades.

You know, a resurrection body can be a very unnerving thing. One minute I'm entirely absorbed in the healing powers of rosemary (it's a wound herb – did you know?), and the next my attention is caught by a slight movement and I look up to see him sitting on the end of my bed, resting his chin in his hand, resting his elbow on his knee, watching me.

"It's you!" I say. "Hi!"

"It's a beautiful day," he says. "You could probably turn the light off."

I glance up at the window. While I've had my mind on other things, the sun has risen, and it does indeed appear to be the most glorious day. I flick the light switch off, stop the video, close down everything I have running – goodness, is that the time? – and shut down my computer.

"I'd better get up," I say. This is a hint – as in, "I need some privacy to get dressed, could you push off for a minute?"

"We could go for a walk by the ghyll," he says, "or by the sea, or up in the firehills."

"Can't," I reply. "I'm sorry. That would have been fun, but I promised to meet my friend in Tunbridge Wells. We're going shopping. I'd better get a move on, or I'll miss the train. But you're right, it is a most splendiferous day. Never mind – the train goes right through the countryside; I'll have a good view of the fields and the woods."

"Well, we could walk down to the station?"

I shake my head. "Too late. If I get up right now I can run for the bus and be in time for the 10.53. I'm so sorry. Another day?"

He isn't listening. He can't be listening.

"Wilderness," he says, "is a state of mind, and an adventure of the soul. Inside every human being there are tracts of wilderness beyond imagining. But –" when he fixes me with his eyes like that, I get the feeling I'm meant to pay attention – "to experience wilderness to the full, to have any kind of grasp on what it really is, you do occasionally have to *go outside*. Whatever else wilderness is, it's not something you encounter vicariously, or watch through the window. It's for you personally. For your actual life."

Oh. Right. Point taken. Maybe tomorrow?

Day 19

Third Sunday in Lent

Luke 2:36–37 NIV

There was also a prophet, Anna, the daughter of Penuel, of the tribe of Asher. She was very old; she had lived with her husband seven years after her marriage, and then was a widow until she was eighty-four. She never left the temple but worshipped night and day, fasting and praying.

Matthew 4:1–4 NIV

Then Jesus was led by the Spirit into the wilderness to be tempted by the devil. After fasting for forty days and forty nights, he was hungry. The tempter came to him and said, "If you are the Son of God, tell these stones to become bread."

Jesus answered, "It is written: 'Man shall not live on bread alone, but on every word that comes from the mouth of God.'"

I think if I'd realized I was going to be spending so much time with Jesus this Lent I might have thought a bit harder about practising some kind of Lenten discipline – giving something up or cutting something out. It's all a bit late for that now.

"I never really got the point of fasting," I say, as we walk down the steep hill to the sea after church, and cross the road to go along the prom. I'm not sure this is an entirely good idea, because the wind is fr-fr-freeeeezing. Jesus has his shoulders hunched against the cold, and he's wearing a rough woollen extra thing – like a shawl or a blanket. I should think he needs it.

He turns his face towards me, and the brown skin has a bloom of cold on it. He looks pinched and chilled.

"Why don't we go into Plenty for a coffee?"

He nods gratefully at this suggestion, so that's what we do. I have a cappuccino, and Jesus has the biggest mug of hot chocolate they do. That answers one question, then – Jesus doesn't give up chocolate for Lent!

"Are you hungry?" I ask him. "Would you like a piece of cake too?"

Yes, he would.

Watching Jesus dispatch a hefty slab of excellent carrot cake reminds me of my original thought. "Fasting," I say, "what's the point?"

"There's no point in fasting," says Jesus. I feel my eyebrows lifting in surprise. "Excuse me," he adds (he was speaking with his mouth full).

"Would you like to explain that to me?" I ask him.

He looks warmer and more relaxed now. He wraps his hands round the mug of chocolate. "Fasting is only to allow you to concentrate, to clear the ground for something else," he says. "It makes you more clear-headed, more focused. If you're fasting for some medical reason it's to remove the complication of the digestive process, to let the physician get a better picture, or give a fever the chance to subside. If you're fasting for prayer it's to allow yourself to become entirely centred on the Father, eye to eye, no distractions. If you're fasting for some special intention or intercession it permits a total one-pointed application of your soul, staying there, holding on, until you achieve what you set out to do."

He drinks some of his chocolate. "It sets you free, too," he adds. "If you can fast, and wait, and pray, it's harder for circumstances to jerk you around. Physical appetite can get to be something of an idol, keeping your attention when there are really more important things to be doing. But other than that there's no point in fasting at all. If you can get to the place where all you are is completely focused on the Father, there's no need to fast any more."

"Self-denial –" (this is starting to be a confession now) "– has never been my strong point. I get tired and discouraged so easily. Being warm, and having something nice to eat, sleeping in a comfy bed and curling up with a hot drink to watch a programme on the telly – well, I know it shouldn't matter to me as much as it does, but these are the things that keep me going. I'm not really cut out for self-denial."

Jesus nods. "Yep," he says, "that's what self-denial *means*."

I think of him in the desert. Was it freezing cold at night? Did the wind blow relentlessly like today? I think of him persevering until he was famished, bringing his entire being to focus in one-pointed attention on the voice of the Father in his heart, calling him, guiding him, preparing him.

I think of the sly tempting of the devil, the suave suggestive voice talking to him about stones that looked almost like bread… "If you *are* the Son of God… all you need to do is tell these stones… bread… bread… bread…"

What must it be like, to live with such power, to practise such forbearance?

"I tell you what," I say, "if it had been me out there in the desert being tempted by Satan, he wouldn't have had to ask me twice. And if I'd gone forty days and nights with nothing – *nothing* – to eat, I wouldn't have stopped at anything half as abstemious as bread. Not me. I'd have turned those stones into cream doughnuts – a whole big plateful."

Jesus looks at me thoughtfully. "Yes," he says, "I can believe it."

Day 20

Monday of Week 4

John 12:24–26 NIV

"Very truly I tell you, unless a grain of wheat falls to the ground and dies, it remains only a single seed. But if it dies, it produces many seeds. Anyone who loves their life will lose it, while anyone who hates their life in this world will keep it for eternal life. Whoever serves me must follow me; and where I am, my servant also will be."

Some people's gardens can be a sort of wilderness. Ours can. You should see when there's been a wet June when the broad beans get going and the peas, and the marrow plants are getting into their stride and the perpetual spinach is up – and the *potatoes*; oh man! Like a forest! Not to mention the weeds, which do very well in all the compost we make out of our veggie scraps. If you were about three years old – or even just a rather short adult – you could easily feel you'd got lost in some untouched valley in the Amazon Basin. The word "primaeval" comes easily to mind.

But right now everything is calmer than that – austere even. The daffodils are out and the bluebells are in leaf but not in flower yet, and we have some glorious tulips. The herbs are all sprouting vigorously; but everything is still calm. It's later on that wild rioting "Go! Go! Go!" phase comes on the scene, and I'll be staggering up and down the path with cans of water from the house roof rain we harvested in our bevy of water butts (700 litres' capacity in all) during the summer, satisfying the thirst of plants that have flowers and leaves to support and night after night of fresh vegetables for our supper growing on their stems and vines and out of sight in the earth beneath our feet.

At the moment the seeds are still here in the shed in their packets. The wind from the sea blows across this hilltop, and our garden is a cold, wild place in March. We don't sow early. But the seed potatoes are on the shelf under the window in the shed, where they can start sprouting, ready to go in the ground in a week or two. We follow tradition and plant them on Good Friday. I mean, we go to chapel on that day of course – but we find time to put the potatoes in as well. We plant them in trenches, the earth piled up between the rows, because you have to earth them up three times as they grow. When the first leaves come up we cover them from the heaped earth alongside the trenches. They grow through that and we cover them again – and now the potato patch looks flat. The third time we cover them and now the hills run along where the potatoes are growing and the valleys lie in-between. And then we let them be.

I show him the seed packets, with the photos on the fronts that together make a collage of English summer – carrots and beetroot, but also sweet peas and snap dragons, love in the mist and night scented stocks, and nasturtiums which will be like having our own Van Gogh painted garden. Nasturtiums look and taste brilliant in a salad.

"Unless a seed fall into the ground and die…" I look at him sidelong and feel sadness and awe that he got to be the seed – the one that died to bring hope to life again for the whole human race, the harvest of salvation. But here it comes again, the same teaching – that *I* must fall into the ground and die as well, let go of everything, be lost from sight and fall into cold darkness and death. "Whoever serves me must follow me," he says; and, "Anyone who loves their life will lose it, while anyone who hates their life in this world will keep it for eternal life." But I do love my life – well not all the time, I've had some rough patches, but I'm not ready to suffer and die.

Then he says, no, that's not it. He picks up a nasturtium seed from the little stash I have hoarded there, lying in the curve of a piece of broken flowerpot up on the shelf.

"This seed," he says, "what is it? It's something and nothing. It's hard and dry, withered and dead. It has no meaning and no beauty, until it's planted. All the life and the joy and the colour and vitality come from burying it in the earth and letting it give up its substance in favour of life. That's what it's *for*."

"I know," I tell him. "But me? Me to die and give up everything? I'm not like a nasturtium. I care."

He smiles. "You're confusing what belongs to life and love in yourself with what can be let go, what can fall into the ground to be a seed. That's normal. Most people do. The important thing is to learn to notice and understand – to learn to see and discern. Anything of which you can say the word 'my' is for planting. 'My career, my health, my opinion, my rights, my ambitions, my savings.' These things, they have their time in your life – they sprout and develop and mature. But they also wither, because they are not life. They grow on and in the ground of your life, but you cannot hang onto them. If you do that, you will have invested your hopes in something that can only die, because that is its nature. Each of these things, once their day has gone, becomes no more than this little nasturtium seed, a dusty, wizened thing. So it is when someone clings on to their money or their position or their status. It had its day and its place in their life, but if they mistake it for life itself, then they will be left with a handful of hard, wizened, shrivelled, dusty little hopes, dead dreams. It's when you let go of them, let them fall, that hope can spring again."

"What?" I say. "So I should pack in my job and just *be*? Give all my money away and just hope for the best?"

He drops the nasturtium seed back carefully onto the pile ready for planting. "All I'm saying," he says quietly, "is you can realize these things come and go, and learn to know the difference between their fleeting forms and the life that underlies them – the real you which comes from the breath of God."

Day 21

Tuesday of Week 4

Mark 10:21–22 NIV

Jesus looked at him and loved him. "One thing you lack," he said. "Go, sell everything you have and give to the poor, and you will have treasure in heaven. Then come, follow me."

At this the man's face fell. He went away sad, because he had great wealth.

It's too cold for sitting out, but the day is so fresh and bright, so we go walking, following the paths down through the park towards the sea. Everywhere around new small plants are shooting with that vivid brightness of early green, but still the trees are bare of leaves. Some of our best conversations are walking ones. Thoughts flow when we move. But I am still stuck in yesterday, still trying to understand what must be taken literally and what is only figurative; what I have to give up and what I'm allowed to keep.

He looks at me sideways. "None of it's figurative," he says. "It's all to be taken literally."

"Now, I don't think you mean that," I reply. "You aren't thinking of the implications of what you're saying." I know, I know. That might not have been the most respectful thing ever said to Jesus – but I'm getting frustrated here.

We keep walking, and he says nothing. When Jesus doesn't speak, I don't feel the tensions that pull in so many silences – like adhesions attaching to internal organs, a kind of disease. The silence that surrounds Jesus when he doesn't speak is like a drop of clear water hanging from a tap. Completely clean and plain. He is just waiting for me to go on with what I'm saying, not muddying the water with irritation and antagonism of his own (I've got enough for both of us – he knows that).

"That rich young man in the gospel stories," I explain. "He had to give away all his money because he loved his money. But some of your friends had money – they must have done, there were enough of you. Twelve hungry men plus yourself all dropping by for supper – are you telling me that hospitality was accomplished without any money?"

"Well," he replies, "they gave it away. They gave what they had to us. They didn't hold on to it."

I digest this thought. "You're right, of course," I say eventually; and then I can't resist adding, "Isn't that the point of being Jesus?" He doesn't look amused.

"I hope not," he says. "Because being right is just one more form of currency. It has no life in it, only competition, having and getting at someone else's expense. For me to be called 'right' someone else has to be 'wrong', and that's a dismal game with no winners.

"But that man you're talking about – the rich man. People come to me for healing, but they don't always read their own symptoms correctly. Oftentimes the reason they need help is because the system they're applying at the moment isn't working. It doesn't make them happy, or well. And they come to me because they're ill and miserable, but my remedies surprise them. That young man came to me hungering and thirsting for life. 'How do I do it?' he wanted to know: 'How can I come into eternal life?' He wanted what I had. What I had was nothing – that was the point.

"So then I saw that his problem was double vision."

"What?" At this point I interrupt. "It says nothing about the rich young man being visually impaired in my version of Mark's Gospel. Is that true?"

He pauses, not to recover his thoughts but to give me a chance to go on protesting – I do like to warm to my subject. But seeing I'm done, he goes on: "When someone has double vision, they have difficulty telling which is the real thing and which is just image. Life gets confusing, and tiring. You reach out for something and find yourself grasping for an illusion."

"And this man had double vision? What did that have to do with his money?"

"Well, as you go about your daily life, whatever you focus on grows. Where you put your attention, you see increase. And this man's problem lay in keeping two things at once before his eyes, one of them real and the other an illusion. He focused on eternal life, but he focused on money as well, and the combination was making him dizzy. He was having trouble telling which was the reality and which was the illusion. I think you know, a lot of people suffer from this problem. Some people even think the spiritual realm is the illusion – I expect you know the term 'airy fairy'. They think money is real – 'hard cash'."

At this point he starts to laugh, taken with the comical thought of people having their ideas so ludicrously upside down. He glances at me to see if I think it's funny too. I try.

"The only way of healing that man, of giving him peace," he continues then, "was to remove the illusion from his field of vision so he could focus in peace on what he really yearned for – eternal life, which *is* reality."

He pauses – another drop of clear, perfect silence forming.

"Those other people – the ones who looked after us," he says softly, with a tenderness of memory in his voice that reaches right to the heart of me, "well, they weren't really thinking about money. That wasn't what they had their attention on. They only knew they loved us and wanted to welcome us. So there was no need for them to give all of it away – or what they had left of it after they'd bought all that bread and cheese and wine and dates and whatnot – because they already knew what was real. They didn't have double vision."

"Oh, I see what you mean." Light dawns. "You mean he was conflicted in his ambitions. He didn't really have double vision."

The air around us is fresh and clear. The fluting song of a bird arises from a tree into the blueness of the sky as we pass beneath.

"Yes. He did," says Jesus.

Day 22

Wednesday of Week 4

Jeremiah 25:8–12 RSV

Therefore thus says the Lord of hosts: Because you have not obeyed my words, behold, I will send for all the tribes of the north, says the Lord, and for Nebuchadrezzar the king of Babylon, my servant, and I will bring them against this land and its inhabitants, and against all these nations round about; I will utterly destroy them, and make them a horror, a hissing, and an everlasting reproach. Moreover, I will banish from them the voice of mirth and the voice of gladness, the voice of the bridegroom and the voice of the bride, the grinding of the millstones and the light of the lamp. This whole land shall become a ruin and a waste, and these nations shall serve the king of Babylon seventy years. Then after seventy years are completed, I will punish the king of Babylon and that nation, the land of the Chaldeans, for their iniquity, says the Lord, making the land an everlasting waste.

Genesis 3:17–18 RSV, God curses Adam

"… cursed is the ground because of you; in toil you shall eat of it all the days of your life; thorns and thistles it shall bring forth to you …"

Exodus 3:7–8 RSV

*Then the Lord said, "I have seen the affliction of my people
who are in Egypt, and have heard their cry because of their
taskmasters; I know their sufferings, and I have come down to
deliver them out of the hand of the Egyptians, and to bring them
up out of that land to a good and broad land, a land flowing
with milk and honey…"*

Isaiah 5:8 RSV

*Woe to those who join house to house, who add field to field,
until there is no more room, and you are made to dwell alone in
the midst of the land.*

Deuteronomy 24:19–21 RSV

*When you reap your harvest in your field, and have forgotten
a sheaf in the field, you shall not go back to get it; it shall
be for the sojourner, the fatherless, and the widow; that the
Lord your God may bless you in all the work of your hands.
When you beat your olive trees, you shall not go over the
boughs again; it shall be for the sojourner, the fatherless, and
the widow. When you gather the grapes of your vineyard, you
shall not glean it afterward; it shall be for the sojourner, the
fatherless, and the widow.*

"When I was a child, I thought the wilderness must be
seriously horrible – a nasty, grim, dangerous, hostile place
that any sane person would avoid. John the Baptist sounded
scary, and when you went into the wilderness, who should you
meet but the devil himself? I got the impression the wilderness
must be one short remove from hell.

"It took me by surprise when I began to read about green
issues, to find that we actually *need* the wilderness – that our
life depends on it. The rainforests, the cloud forests, the Arctic

ice cap, the wetlands. The Bible makes wilderness sound dreadful – but it's really good – isn't it?"

Jesus smiles. "Well… it's to do with balance – the rhythm of going out and returning home; like breathing in and out, like the ebb tide and the flow tide. And it's about point of view. The word 'wilderness' is itself a point of view – to the monkey, the tiger, the eagle, the snake, wilderness isn't wilderness, it's home. To them, wilderness is the cage with only a picture of trees and rocks, the concrete enclosure with a pool of tap water and a painting of the sky. In the forest or the craggy mountains where stranded humans feel so afraid and alone, the wild creatures know their freedom and are content. But even humans love the wild places that have been left in peace."

"So the balance is… what? Taking some and leaving some?" I pick up a pine cone fallen in the grass around the bench where we are sitting at the side of the path, and turn it over in my hands, looking at its structure and colour.

"The balance," he says, "is that people need to cultivate the land: to farm crops and animals, to build homes and hospitals, marketplaces, shops and places of worship, roads and playgrounds – everything that makes up civilization. But at the same time blessing flows from taking only what they need, from living humbly and simply and keeping close to the earth. Consumerism, growth economics – they are not sustainable, which is another way of saying they do not belong to blessing. Something not sustainable is tending towards death. Blessing tends towards life."

"So – wilderness good, farming good, even whole towns full of houses and factories good – but taking the whole lot until there's nothing left for anyone else and the land can't renew itself, bad? Fracking and tar sands and cutting down the rainforest to grow palm groves for bio-diesel, bad? Wars caused by displacing people from their traditional homes so we can have it for beef ranches to make the mega-burgers that give us heart disease, bad? Free range chickens in the woodland, good; vast stinking closed barns of chickens crammed into wire cages under artificial light their whole life long, bad?"

"I'd have said that was self-evident," says Jesus.

Day 23

Thursday of Week 4

Mark 6:1–6 GNT

Jesus left that place and went back to his hometown, followed by his disciples. On the Sabbath he began to teach in the synagogue. Many people were there; and when they heard him, they were all amazed. "Where did he get all this?" they asked. "What wisdom is this that has been given him? How does he perform miracles? Isn't he the carpenter, the son of Mary, and the brother of James, Joseph, Judas, and Simon? Aren't his sisters living here?" And so they rejected him.

Jesus said to them, "Prophets are respected everywhere except in their own hometown and by their relatives and their family."

He was not able to perform any miracles there, except that he placed his hands on a few sick people and healed them. He was greatly surprised, because the people did not have faith.

John 1:10–11 GNT

The Word was in the world, and though God made the world through him, yet the world did not recognize him. He came to his own country, but his own people did not receive him.

"I like walking," I say to Jesus as we climb the hill together, through the damp darkness of this cold and exceedingly dismal evening, on our way to the church meeting. "All my shoes are walking shoes. I haven't got one fancy pair left – by which I mean the sort you only wear for show but they pinch and give you blisters. Everywhere in this town is so far away from everywhere else that I'd be spending a fortune on bus fares if I had shoes that hurt my feet. Anyway, walking's good for us. I saw a video on the internet about some man who lost a huge amount of weight just by walking every day – he didn't go especially fast, he just kept going. And I like walking."

"Good," says Jesus. "I like walking too. But what you are not saying is…?"

I suppose you already know this, but there is not much mileage in trying to keep anything hidden from Jesus.

"Well… it just sounds so unreasonable," I mumble.

"Uh-huh? What does?"

So I tell him. "Most of the people who go to church meetings have cars. If I call them and ask for a lift, they are always gracious and kind, they willingly take me. At least – most of the time. If it's not too far out of their way. But they mostly don't remember that I haven't got a car. They don't call me and ask if I'd like a lift. They don't volunteer to set up an arrangement where they would come by for me. In the summertime that's no problem at all. But in the winter when it's dark and cold and wet, I'd just love it if, without having to ask, they offered. It's hard to ask. And, if I'm honest, half the time when it's not actually tipping it down with rain, it's not the walking that's the problem. It's knowing that, in a car culture, if people don't offer you a lift that means they don't care about you."

Jesus listens to this. I glance at him. "It makes all the difference in the world," I add, "walking along to the meeting with you. It's like that thing G. K. Chesterton said in *The Man Who Was Thursday*: '… there are no words to express the abyss between isolation and having one ally… two is not twice one; two is two thousand times one'. Having someone to go with makes it into something I actually want to do. I know I should feel enthusiastic about it anyway, because the meetings are about spreading the gospel and building the kingdom. But if the people I'm meant to be doing it with don't care if I'm there or not, then I start to not care either. And it's not far from that to not wanting to go at all. So – thank you for walking to church with me tonight. Thank you so much."

"Well," says Jesus, "I understand about being the odd one out. About not fitting in."

Yes. He surely does. More than I do. As we come over the crest of the hill and start down the other side towards the sea, I think about the stable at Bethlehem, where there was no room at the inn; and how the people from Nazareth shunned him because his teaching was so wise and holy that they thought he was getting above himself. I think about Judas, his friend, betraying him for cash to people who wanted to kill him. And about all the religious establishment men who unabashedly wanted him dead. And Pilate who thought it seemed a pity, but not enough to intervene. He just signed the death warrant.

How strange, that someone who came for the precise purpose of being with us – Emmanuel, God with us – was not actually wanted when he got here.

The most scary part of the desert is that it can feel so lonely. Going into the wilderness with a friend turns an ordeal into an adventure – what you were afraid of starts to be fun. Well – perhaps not if you're going to be fasting for forty days, but in general, I mean.

And even things that were meant to be fun, like parties and quiz nights, can be an ordeal if no one cares about you and you're all by yourself. Maybe that's what wilderness is – a place no one cares about, ground nobody has loved. The cultivation of kindness changes everything.

Day 24

Friday of Week 4

Acts 16:22–26 NRSV

*The crowd joined in attacking them, and the magistrates
had them stripped of their clothing and ordered them to be
beaten with rods. After they had given them a severe flogging,
they threw them into prison and ordered the jailer to keep
them securely. Following these instructions, he put them in
the innermost cell and fastened their feet in the stocks. About
midnight Paul and Silas were praying and singing hymns to
God, and the prisoners were listening to them. Suddenly there
was an earthquake, so violent that the foundations of the prison
were shaken; and immediately all the doors were opened and
everyone's chains were unfastened.*

2 Corinthians 12:8–10 GNT

*Three times I prayed to the Lord about this and asked him to
take it away. But his answer was: "My grace is all you need,
for my power is greatest when you are weak." I am most happy,
then, to be proud of my weaknesses, in order to feel the protection
of Christ's power over me. I am content with weaknesses,
insults, hardships, persecutions, and difficulties for Christ's sake.
For when I am weak, then I am strong.*

Luke 22:42 GNT

*"Father," he said, "if you will, take this cup of suffering away
from me. Not my will, however, but your will be done."*

Luke 23:34 GNT

Jesus said, "Forgive them, Father! They don't know what they are doing."

"I'm not too sure my prayer is working," I say doubtfully. "I don't really know what we're going to do."

He stops and looks at me. "Not working?" he says. "How do you mean?"

"Well…" I'm taken aback by this reply. What's not to understand in "not working"? "Well… we haven't seen any improvement in her condition, the prognosis isn't good, and if they can't get her bloods right in very short order then she won't be able to have the op at all."

"Oh, right." He sets off walking again.

"Can you say a bit more?" My gaze questions his. "Am I doing it wrong?"

He shakes his head. "It doesn't matter so much what you say. Father hears the love. Your prayer opens the connections for light to shine through. But prayer isn't primarily about outcomes and situations. It's an orientation of the soul. About aligning yourself with the flow of grace in the world, so that you watch what the Father is doing, and do nothing else except that. Things are as they are. What is, just is. The question is how you respond. The ability to respond – responsibility. Prayer is accepting responsibility for what comes into your life – embracing it. Responsibility confers authority, and it's also accountability. Are you with me?"

I shake my head. No. "Er… not really. Can you run that by me again?"

I love it when this happens. He looks at me, and instead of irritation clouding his face because I am so slow, he is suddenly lit up with a grin like unexpected sunburst. Not mocking me, I mean – just as though… well, as though he is my friend.

"When something comes before your attention, you respond. Or, to put it another way, you become responsible for it – same thing. Nothing happens in isolation. The way things are – it's always part of the whole interconnected web of life, the pattern of love woven by the Spirit of truth. If you give a little tug at any circumstance, if you dislodge anything, you change the whole pattern, because everything is connected. Everything is part of everything else, and that of course includes you. But you cannot be responsible for everything and everybody – you would become swamped and overwhelmed. You are asked only to be responsible for yourself and what is in front of you – to love your neighbour as yourself. So you choose how you will respond to every circumstance you meet. You look puzzled."

"Can you give me an example?" I ask.

"Sure. Take this afternoon, when we waited forty-five minutes in the cold wind for a bus that didn't turn up. When it finally arrived and you said to the bus driver how long you'd been waiting, and he was so rude to you; let's think about that, and about loving your neighbour as yourself. The first circumstance was waiting. The cold – you can get resentful and indignant and impatient, and start thinking about how often the bus is late and what you're going to say to that driver when he gets there – or you can just possess your soul in patience and wait peacefully; or call a cab if you feel you've waited long enough and you have the money. And you can tell the Father, just quietly in your mind, how you feel. If you can't enjoy what's happening, you can accept it. Then when the bus gets there, you are confronted with the driver, so now you have responsibility for him – he is your neighbour now. To look at him with the love that everyone needs. Not to blame him. To ask quietly and without drama what happened to make him so late, and if he's all right. So he knows he has been received by love. After all, you can't make it any earlier or less cold; but you can make it loving. How you speak to him, look at him, will affect the whole web of life – how he drives, how he feels when he gets home… What is, is. You choose your response; you take responsibility."

"And my friend – who is so ill?"

He looks at me seriously. "Father knows her and loves her. Her times are in his hands. But she is your responsibility – you can tell, because she is in your life. So you choose carefully how to respond, how to love her. You hold her in the light as you walk in the light; you keep her with you. You abide in me, and I abide in you, and our love flows along the web to her. And this must be so, because all things are connected. All you have to do is take responsibility, for loving and for living in the light. There is no such thing as a prayer that doesn't work. Prayer is mega. It changes everything. It's the juice that runs the whole system."

Day 25

Saturday of Week 4

Jeremiah 19:14 – 20:6 NRSV

When Jeremiah came from Topheth, where the Lord had sent him to prophesy, he stood in the court of the Lord's house and said to all the people: Thus says the Lord of hosts, the God of Israel: I am now bringing upon this city and upon all its towns all the disaster that I have pronounced against it, because they have stiffened their necks, refusing to hear my words.

Now the priest Pashhur son of Immer, who was chief officer in the house of the Lord, heard Jeremiah prophesying these things. Then Pashhur struck the prophet Jeremiah, and put him in the stocks that were in the upper Benjamin Gate of the house of the Lord. The next morning when Pashhur released Jeremiah from the stocks, Jeremiah said to him, The Lord has named you not Pashhur but "Terror-all-around." For thus says the Lord: I am making you a terror to yourself and to all your friends; and they shall fall by the sword of their enemies while you look on. And I will give all Judah into the hand of the king of Babylon; he shall carry them captive to Babylon, and shall kill them with the sword. I will give all the wealth of this city, all its gains, all its prized belongings, and all the treasures of the kings of Judah into the hand of their enemies, who shall plunder them, and seize them, and carry them to Babylon. And you, Pashhur, and all who live in your house, shall go into captivity, and to Babylon you shall go; there you shall die, and there you shall be buried, you and all your friends, to whom you have prophesied falsely.

Isaiah 45:6–7 NRSV

I am the Lord, and there is no other. I form light and create
darkness, I make weal and create woe; I the Lord do all these
things.

"For a long time," I say, as we lean on the railings looking
out across the moody, restless sea under the violet burden of
clouds, "I think people were mainly afraid of God. Scared of
his displeasure, of hell and damnation. Then came a preaching
revolution, underlining his loving kindness. Adrian Plass spoke
reassurance to the hearts of an anxious generation, saying, 'God
is nice, and he likes you.' But I wonder… you see… I've been
surprised by how many of the people I know seem to think the
existence of God *at all* is synonymous with 'things going well
for me'. Someone they love gets cancer, a lunatic goes crazy in
a playground with a gun, they're made redundant in a time of
recession and can't get another job – and before you know it
they're concluding there was never any God after all. As if God
is a commodity or a personal accessory or something – like an
application you can download to make the workings of life run
more smoothly. I've listened to people give testimony in church,
saying, 'God is really important in my life', and I think, what the
hey? What does that mean? A little God that can be fitted into
my big important life, there in the corner, helpfully making all
the difference. But God… well, God is foundational to reality.
Reality *means* what proceeds from God. He is the source of the
big picture, underlying the meta-narrative, the plane on which
all life vibrates. So I do wonder, reading some of the stuff in the
Bible issuing dire warnings to people to change their ways or get
ready for trouble, if that's not so much God having a hissy fit as
the prophet articulating the inevitable. This is what happens if
you try to fly in the face of the reality God has ordained. You
muck up bigtime. It all ends in tears. The whole bang shoot

comes crashing down around you. And that's not divine spite; it's the plain mechanism of how life is made to be."

Jesus listens to this.

"Have I… have I got that right?" I ask him. He considers. Something I notice about Jesus is that he never rushes in. He waits, and thinks. He weighs his words. And he listens properly. Half the time in a conversation I'm waiting with contained impatience for the other person to stop speaking so I can have my turn and spit out the words queuing up inside my head. But that doesn't seem to be how Jesus does conversation. He pays attention. He stays in the now.

"The Father's love," he says then, "is big enough to embrace the worst that can befall us; holding it until it develops into blessing. His love is like a matrix that transfigures everything put through it. Death and pain, loss and sorrow, injustice and bewilderment and longing – when these are held in the Father's love and surrender to its power, everything yields blessing. There is no limit to this – of time or space. However far gone a situation, nothing is beyond redemption. Even the challenges of global proportions. There is no shelf life to his love's transformative power, no place his touch cannot reach to save. And his judgment, his wrath – yes, it is terrifying. It shakes the heavens and the foundations of the earth – because that's what it takes. His judgment is the dark face of his love. This is impenetrable to human thought, which longs for comfort, for sunshine, wanting everything to proceed evenly. Nobody asks for a bumpy ride. And at times, when a person gets caught up in the purposes of God's love, it gets to the stage where you've just had enough, feel you can't take any more of this, cry out at the end of your tether, 'Is there honestly no other way to do this? Must I really drink this bitter draught right to the dregs?' But the terror, the pain, the dread even – these are the mystery of love."

Gosh. Okay.

"Not the Devil attacking?"

Jesus sighs. He doesn't look irritated or impatient. More like inside him there is this great big vision – insight, maybe, something he can see and I can't – that is just so hard to get across.

"The Devil," he says quietly, "has no dominion. The sting of death is drawn. There is only love, now; but it may sometimes take everything you have."

He looks up at the wild sky as the first big raindrops start to fall.

Day 26

Laetare Sunday

Lamentations 1:1–2 GNT

How lonely lies Jerusalem, once so full of people!
Once honoured by the world, she is now like a widow;
The noblest of cities has fallen into slavery.
All night long she cries; tears run down her cheeks.
Of all her former friends, not one is left to comfort her.
Her allies have betrayed her and are all against her now.

Isaiah 49:13–16 GNT

The Lord will comfort his people; he will have pity on his
suffering people.

But the people of Jerusalem said, "The Lord has abandoned
us! He has forgotten us."

So the Lord answers, "Can a woman forget her own baby and
not love the child she bore? Even if a mother should forget her child,
I will never forget you. Jerusalem, I can never forget you! I have
written your name on the palms of my hands."

Matthew 24:9–12 NRSV

"Then they will hand you over to be tortured and will put you to
death, and you will be hated by all nations because of my name.
Then many will fall away, and they will betray one another and
hate one another. And many false prophets will arise and lead
many astray. And because of the increase of lawlessness, the love
of many will grow cold.

Lamentations 3:22–24 NRSV

The steadfast love of the Lord never ceases, his mercies never come to an end; they are new every morning; great is your faithfulness.

"The Lord is my portion," says my soul, "therefore I will hope in him."

I walk back moodily from church. I hate that story about Hannah dropping off the infant Samuel at the Temple – the one in the first chapter of the first book of Samuel, that we always have on Mother's Day. I hate the idea of abandoning a toddler to be brought up by an old man in a great big religious building. I'm still brooding on it.

"You know what I really can't stand? Children being left to cry. This poisonous 'cry it out' trend in raising children, where a toddler is left in a dark room alone, locked in, crying helplessly, as a means of teaching him to sleep through the night. Or the child who is picked on by the adults to whom God entrusted him; humiliated and punished, harassed and frightened. It's like an epidemic of heart disease, soul sickness. As though compassion has rotted and mercy has died.

"Abandonment, betrayal – these are so terrible to experience. They drive us out into a wilderness where we can see no mercy, no hope. They create some of the most arid, lonely, conditions in all the earth."

Jesus listens to these words spurting out of so deep a place in my soul, his face grave and still.

I don't need him to speak, to agree or comfort, because I know that he knows all about abandonment and betrayal. The kiss of Judas. I think of that deathly kiss, its falsity striking like hard frost burning and desiccating, cauterizing the living tissue of the human heart. Abandonment and betrayal wither our courage, stop our joy. With a steadfast companion a pilgrim can meet adversity dauntlessly; abandoned and betrayed, hope withers and grows sere.

I think of a man who worked hard to support his family, never imagining the wife he trusted to care for his home and children was having an affair with his best friend. I think of the politicians who promised so much before the elections – to protect the earth, to care for the sick, to lift children out of poverty; and I look at their hard eyes and fleshy faces in the seat of power, rewarding the rich and abandoning the poor like a used rag. I think of little girls raped and trafficked, and my heart breaks for their trampled innocence.

"Jesus..." I say; "Jesus... why is the world like this? Oh, what can we do? How can we heal it? However can we even start to put right such a spreading cold of indifference?"

He nods, understanding. Jesus will not offer me glib answers or slick solutions. He feels the swelling of my sorrow into this silence.

"The only way I know," he says after a while, "is to go – to go yourself. What you cannot stop, you can at least share. And – if you share in somebody's abandonment, then they are no longer alone. If you stand with someone who has been betrayed, you restore faithfulness to their lives."

"*What?*" This appals me. "You are joking! *Me?* What can *I* do? I can't stop sex trafficking and child abuse and divorce – I mean, look, I'm divorced myself! Where did *I* get it right? I'm not cut out for politics and I haven't got the money to free slaves!"

I glare at him. He meets my gaze steadily.

"Well..." I admit after a moment, "I guess I can buy fair-traded groceries, and high welfare meat and free-range woodland eggs. I guess I can manage a small donation at least for the street children. I suppose I can take the trouble to visit my mother so that as she grows old and sees the friends of a lifetime dying one by one, she doesn't feel too unbearably lonely.

I could write a letter to a prisoner. I could sign my name to a petition against human trafficking. Things like that, I could manage; the little things."

And this makes Jesus smile.

Day 27

Monday of Week 5

Genesis 1:27–28 NIV

So God created mankind in his own image,
in the image of God he created them;
male and female he created them.
God blessed them and said to them, "Be fruitful and increase in
number; fill the earth and subdue it. Rule over the fish in the sea
and the birds in the sky and over every living creature that moves
on the ground."

Colossians 1:15–20 NIV

The Son is the image of the invisible God, the firstborn over all
creation. For in him all things were created: things in heaven
and on earth, visible and invisible, whether thrones or powers
or rulers or authorities; all things have been created through
him and for him. He is before all things, and in him all things
hold together. And he is the head of the body, the church; he is
the beginning and the firstborn from among the dead, so that in
everything he might have the supremacy. For God was pleased to
have all his fullness dwell in him, and through him to reconcile
to himself all things, whether things on earth or things in heaven,
by making peace through his blood, shed on the cross.

The most magnificent wilderness of my personal experience
has to be the ocean. Hidden, inscrutable, undeclared, all life is
there – much of it incomprehensibly alien. Even the bit we can

see, just the top of it, is wild enough. In the autumn and now in the spring come the great tides of the equinox, sand-gold waves frothed with lace like an out-of-control diva all sound and fury and heaving breast, flinging stuff everywhere and wreaking havoc.

High on the cliff here we look towards the path of light streaming across the water from the sinking sun. Heavy clouds underlit with vermilion glory mass in the west.

I think of Jesus, tossing in the fishing boat on Lake Galilee, fast asleep while his friends, seasoned sailors, begin to panic; getting up drowsy and slightly annoyed at being disturbed, to chide the foaming sea. From his rebuke proceeds peace. I consider what this means, to hold such dominion.

"The waves and the wind," I remark, "they did what you said. Amazing. That's so amazing."

"It is the trust of humankind," he answers me simply, "to subdue the earth. It is God's command to us, our charge to fulfil."

"To have dominion over the earth? I have friends who say that climate change is nonsense, that we can do what we like to the earth because when everything is fulfilled God will make a new heaven and a new earth so this one is kinda disposable. They say God gave us the earth to do what we like with. A resource, I guess. Just, *ours*. So it doesn't matter if the tigers die out and the frankincense trees. It doesn't matter if we drill up the Arctic wilderness for oil, and cut down the trees of the cloud forest. What matters is the human economy. Actually, even saying it aloud I can't imagine how anybody could think that way and not notice how colossally stupid it is. Because we all belong to one another, don't we? Not only the human family, I mean, but the whole web of creation."

He listens, looking out across the splendour of the sea. I can't begin to tell you how comforting it is, to have Jesus listen to you. Just to talk to him. There is a sanity in his presence, an intelligence, that gives me the feeling that somehow, because he is here with me, whatever happens everything will be all right in the end. Like his friends in the boat, storm-flung – any kind of apocalypse scenario could conceivably be brought to heel by the quality of his presence.

"Dominion…" he murmurs, "power… Without accountability, these are meaningless. The power to consume and destroy is not God's dominion. God is the creator. From him all life proceeds. But you cannot serve God and Mammon, because no one can be the loyal servant of two different masters. When human decisions and behaviours are driven by the imperatives of economic growth, that is not dominion, it is slavery. Consuming and destroying are not power, only insanity. The reign of God is a peaceable kingdom. Where wholeness comes, and peace, where the delicate perfect balance of life finds the poise of equilibrium, there is the dominion of God. The politics of the human race are conditioned by fear – razor wire along the borders and soldiers with guns; arms fairs and nuclear deterrents, tanks rumbling ominously across the trackless desert. But God did not give humanity this spirit of fear – whether to fear others or to make them afraid. The Spirit of God brings the power not to plunder but to love; not the madness and terror of war but the sound mind of the peacemaker. This rape of the earth is accursed. How could it be otherwise? In the peaceable kingdom, all things hold together. Everything dies, assuredly. All beings have their time to be born and then to pass away. But the one who loves God holds creation sacred – for so it is. The creation is in covenant relationship with the Father.

"And you are amazed when I say 'Peace', and the winds and the waves become calm. But it is only because they can trust the words I say. There is no falsehood in it, you see. Nature can discern falsehood. If a man says 'Peace' and there is no peace in his heart, in his life, the living earth will not pay attention to him.

When he prays for peace while preparing for war, his prayers go nowhere. Man says 'Peace' and woodland creatures everywhere flee for their lives at the sound of his voice. Man protects his peace with a fleet of nuclear warheads trained upon his imagined enemy. He deludes himself, because flesh and blood are never the enemy of humankind, only that which sucks a man's soul dry of all kindness and compassion. Man says 'Peace' and trains every living thing to ignore him. It is his habitual rapacity that has made a miracle of the dominion of God."

In the silence that follows his words, a silence swelling with sadness, we listen to the rhythmic pound and drag of the waves on the shingle, and to the wild cry of wheeling gulls. We watch the last liquid crimson of the sun bleed out across the western sky.

Day 28

Tuesday of Week 5

1 Kings 19:8–13 GNT

Elijah got up, ate and drank, and the food gave him enough strength to walk forty days to Sinai, the holy mountain. There he went into a cave to spend the night.

Suddenly the Lord spoke to him, "Elijah, what are you doing here?"

He answered, "Lord God Almighty, I have always served you – you alone. But the people of Israel have broken their covenant with you, torn down your altars, and killed all your prophets. I am the only one left – and they are trying to kill me!"

"Go out and stand before me on top of the mountain," the Lord said to him. Then the Lord passed by and sent a furious wind that split the hills and shattered the rocks – but the Lord was not in the wind. The wind stopped blowing, and then there was an earthquake – but the Lord was not in the earthquake. After the earthquake there was a fire – but the Lord was not in the fire. And after the fire there was the soft whisper of a voice.

When Elijah heard it, he covered his face with his cloak and went out and stood at the entrance of the cave. A voice said to him, "Elijah, what are you doing here?"

I think it would be fair to say that I have been able to raise procrastinating to a combination of Art Form and Occupation. In my toolkit of strategies for avoiding actually knuckling down to the task awaiting my attention, by far the most useful and durable ruses are eating and buying things.

I wander down to the kitchen to brew a cup of tea, and the five minutes I promised myself extends to baking a whole batch of sticky buns and some leek and potato soup while I'm there. It's surprising how much I can accomplish just as long as I'm really supposed to be doing something else.

And I become spellbound by Facebook trivia and YouTube videos, embroiled in long chats about politics and animal rights. Almost anything seems important while I'm meant to be doing some work. It occurs to me to search out a journal I thought I'd subscribe to, and I remember to look up reviews of barefoot running shoes and make a price comparison on a selection of discount sites.

Strung out, unfocused and almost used up, I return for one last push at half past two in the morning. This article has to be written today. It has to be on the editor's desk when she gets into her office.

The silence of Jesus says, "That, my chum, is the point of fasting in the wilderness."

No internet. No coffee breaks. No shops. No reading material.

Apparently (I read this on Facebook), there's a Muslim tradition of men going into the desert to find themselves again, to recover their real selves that got lost in all the confusion of everyday life. They are known as "men of memory", a title also given to the state historians of the Central African Luba tribe, who were entrusted with committing to memory the cultural minutiae that made up their identity. The men who went out into the magnificent silence of the desert knew that in escaping from distraction they could find themselves again. Free from the attraction of conversations overheard, of news and gossip, free from household problems and squabbles, and from eye-catching pastimes and wares, the refugee from trivial impedimenta finds his mind clarifying into the seeing mirror of the soul.

Tossed about in all the coming and going of daily life, a man captures data and retains detail of current events going on around him. He knows what he had for lunch and what's on TV in the evening, but his mind is filled with the urgent chatter of an incessant procession of stuff that hardly matters. Going cold turkey from all this in the desert is drastic, but it works. The deep dilemmas of his heart, the existential verities, the ontological insights and struggles begin to make themselves felt. As he goes down, down into the unbearable intensity of being, feeling its flimsiness, its immensity, flung between its ennui and its potency, he is left with nowhere to run from what it is to be human. To be alone. In such circumstances, men meet God, and God meets the Devil.

The wilderness is not for wimps. It nails the soul inescapably to the intolerable crux of reality.

The desert as an aid to concentration is unrivalled.

In every walk of life, those who face decisions that really matter, momentous tasks to be undertaken, solemn vows and profound responsibilities, intuitively seek wilderness. They hike in the mountains and walk by the ocean, they book into the hermitage and row out to the island.

Jesus, walking away from the comfortable familiarity of his home at Nazareth, is no exception. The time has come to focus on who he is, and what he has come here to do.

I close down Facebook and put away the interesting journal about land rights. The phone rings but I don't answer it. Downstairs I hear the family laughing and talking, but I stay here as night falls, in the silence of my small room. There is work to be done.

I write sitting on my bed. The room is so little that I can sit at the head of the bed, leaning my back against the wall, and Jesus can sit at the other end with the opposite wall as a back-rest.

His presence is no distraction. I look up from time to time, and there he still is; his eyes are closed and his features composed into a perfect radiance of peace. Jesus, my Lord, is beautiful. His soul encompasses the desert, the ocean, the sky. Even without leaving the confinement of my tiny room I can enter the immensity of this absolute spaciousness. He is praying, I think – praying for me. And I get my work done.

Day 29

Wednesday of Week 5

Psalm 139:1–10 1928 Book of Common Prayer

O Lord, thou hast searched me out, and known me.
Thou knowest my down-sitting, and mine uprising;
*   thou understandest my thoughts long before.*
Thou art about my path, and about my bed;
*   and art acquainted with all my ways.*
For lo, there is not a word in my tongue, but thou,
*   O Lord, knowest it altogether.*
Thou hast beset me behind and before, and laid thine
*   hand upon me.*
Such knowledge is too wonderful and excellent for me;
*   I cannot attain unto it.*
Whither shall I go then from thy Spirit? Or whither shall
*   I go then from thy presence?*
If I climb up into heaven, thou art there; if I go down to
*   hell, thou art there also.*
If I take the wings of the morning, and remain in the uttermost
*   parts of the sea; even there also shall thy hand lead me,*
*   and thy right hand shall hold me.*
If I say, peradventure the darkness shall cover me; then shall
*   my night be turned to day.*
Yea, the darkness is no darkness with thee, but the night is as
*   clear as the day; the darkness and light to thee are*
*   both alike.*

"Jesus?" I say, quietly. "Jesus?"

It is four o'clock in the morning, silent and quite dark. The banks of cloud will have obscured all light from the moon and stars tonight. I think I am alone. But you never know. It's always worth probing the darkness to see, isn't it?

"Jesus?"

And then I know. He is there with me. He is listening. How do I know this, here in the darkness, where no light gives? Because, now I know him, I would know him anywhere. I can feel him near. He is with me. Sharing the particular quality of this darkness, this silence… this night.

"Jesus… I am so angry. So very, very angry."

There is more than one kind of anger. A superficial kind shouts and blusters and swears, slamming doors and crashing things down. This is a different kind of anger. It is a complete rage that so occupies the basement of my being that I feel I could never be free of it. It has grown out of pain long borne, a sense of deep injustice. It feeds on disappointment that verges on despair. I contain it as carefully as I can, because if this blows it will take the whole house with it. No. Make that the street. The town. My world.

"I am so angry."

The dark silence continues for a while. Night silence has a texture, something like microfleece. The silence of night is not silky but furry. It does not have the shine of daytime, the silky slip of twilight silence, the dry cotton silence of the afternoon. For a while I just touch the silence, feeling things ease a little because he is there.

"Would you like to tell me about it?" he asks me, and his voice is quiet in the silence, does not intrude; his words widen silence into a receptive bowl of love – such a surprising thing, that the entire quality of night can be transformed by the presence of love.

So I tell him. About futilities and rejections, about the particular ache of insignificance and invisibility, about the long weary drag of never being able to make anything of this, and not being free to put it down and walk away either. I tell him about chances missed and work ruined, dreams that withered in their spring, the gradual erosion of hope, the slow cold seeping in of meaninglessness. Bitter herbs, the children of Israel ate to remind them of their long walk through the desert. Chewing bitter herbs. The anger was not what I first took it for, a thing of itself. It is a red caul of hide from a skinned life, stretched over a chaos of useless effort. If this were smaller, I would weep for it, but it means too much for that. I can only sit still. There is no life left. Anger was its last flare. No life, no hope, no chance or opportunity. Only me; and Jesus.

I am not sure what I expect him to say. I have grown tired of empty encouragements, of things said to cheer me up and help me look on the bright side. Equally am I tired of blame and criticism when I reach out for something for myself, when I offer my vision, my point of view. What can he say? "Come on, it's not that bad"? "Things'll pick up, you'll see"? Or, worse, "There are plenty of people in much more difficult circumstances than you; you should be grateful." Or, direst of all, "We must put aside all anger, it's not the way of my disciples. Stop it."

This night has become my night, my darkness. Even so, I find my attention shift a little, from complete absorption with the burning core of rage that has got out of hand and begun to consume me, to a curiosity about his response. Jesus?

This is what I did not expect. The silence continues a while longer, and in its continuing the focus of my mind diverts entirely onto him. And in the silence, he reaches across and takes my hand.

Here in the darkness I sit holding the hand of Jesus.

Time passes. At last I fall asleep.

Day 30

Thursday of Week 5

Jeremiah 17:5–8 NRSV

Thus says the Lord:
Cursed are those who trust in mere mortals and make mere flesh
their strength, whose hearts turn away from the Lord.
They shall be like a shrub in the desert, and shall not see when
relief comes.
They shall live in the parched places of the wilderness, in an
uninhabited salt land.
Blessed are those who trust in the Lord, whose trust is the Lord.
They shall be like a tree planted by water, sending out its roots
by the stream.
It shall not fear when heat comes, and its leaves shall stay green;
in the year of drought it is not anxious, and it does not cease to
bear fruit.

Psalm 84:5–7 NRSV

Happy are those whose strength is in you, in whose heart are
the highways to Zion. As they go through the valley of Baca
they make it a place of springs; the early rain also covers it with
pools. They go from strength to strength; the God of gods will be
seen in Zion.

John 4:13–14 NRSV

Jesus said to her, "Everyone who drinks of this water will be
thirsty again, but those who drink of the water that I will give

them will never be thirsty. The water that I will give will become in them a spring of water gushing up to eternal life."

I am trying to get my head round this.

"Do you notice," I ask Jesus, "that wilderness in the Bible seems to have as many layers as an onion? Just when I think I've grasped the concept, I find it has another level!"

He is waiting patiently. Listening. Perhaps I'm not explaining myself very well.

"I mean," I elaborate, "that in the Scriptures wilderness is a physical place – like John the Baptist living in the wilderness. But it works as a metaphor too, even when it *is* physical. So the people of God walking around and around in the wilderness is a physical event with practical considerations attached – getting enough to eat and drink, getting lost, and so on – but it also expresses their spiritual journey: the searching, the lessons learned and forgotten and learned again, going over the same old ground in their journey, as they muddle along towards God. And John the Baptist – his desert home is like a reflection of the untameable, uncompromising, ascetic wild heart he had. Stark prophet, all the way through! See? The outside and the inside are the same!"

I am looking at him eagerly. He smiles. "Yes," he admits, "yes, I had noticed that."

"Good." I am warming to my subject now. "But then there's another layer deeper in. It comes in the psalms a lot. About people going through the valley of Baca – that's a kind of wilderness, right? A harsh, arid, narrow passage?"

"The Bitter Valley," he murmurs, nodding in assent.

"Yes – that one! Well, about people going through that dry, barren place and making it a place of springs, making it fertile; just by their attitude. That people can change their circumstances by changing the attitude they bring to what happens to them.

There's an outside/inside thing going on. Because – get this – as well as affecting what's happing outside them (their circumstances) by their attitude, they can also affect their attitude by immersing themselves in the presence of God: '… like a tree planted by water, sending out its roots by the stream…'

"But… although that's reaching outside themselves for succour and nourishment, it's at that deeper layer; it's an inside sort of outside, a *spiritual* environment not dependent on physical conditions."

Jesus is grinning. I am no theologian, and this is getting plainer by the minute. "I'm doing my best," I protest. "I'm trying to explain!"

"It's okay," he says. "I understand."

I plough on determinedly. "So there's the complete outside – the physical – which is somehow connected with what's inside a person because it mirrors and expresses their inside landscape. Then further in comes the spiritual environment they immerse themselves in, which can be fertile or desert or anything in-between – their choice. But there's a deeper layer still, a place right at the core, which can be almost magical. And that centre is more like a gap, a way through. Like a doorway. *Happy are those whose strength is in you, in whose heart are the highways to Zion* – a road home that runs through the heart and has to be found. Or I suppose it could be just a wandering, an unmarked desert road leading to nowhere. And the gap, the space, at the centre of a person can be just emptiness – a crater, a dust bowl, a black hole of despair everything vanishes into like water going down the plughole – or it can be a well, a spring of life, a place of refreshment. It's a socket, isn't it? An access point. A portal."

I sit, deep in thought, seeing the concentric rings with their opposite possibilities. The space at the very centre, through which life wells up or drains away, through which the road home or the road to exile runs. Then around that an inner context of spiritual landscape, a chosen environment in which the heart is immersed, that is either nourishing or toxic. Then around that, an outer layer of daily life and surroundings, which mirrors and expresses the inner landscape and the choices of the heart.

"What I want to know, though…" I frown in puzzled concentration, "is whether it's a two-way flow. Do the outermost circumstances affect the nature of a person's central reality, or is it always only the heart's core that makes the difference?"

"Circumstances can always be altered," says Jesus. "The important thing is what's in your heart."

Day 31

Friday of Week 5

Psalm 119:130 KJV

The entrance of thy words giveth light; it giveth understanding unto the simple.

1 John 1:5 KJV

This then is the message which we have heard of him, and declare unto you, that God is light, and in him is no darkness at all.

2 Corinthians 4:6 KJV

For God, who commanded the light to shine out of darkness, hath shined in our hearts, to give the light of the knowledge of the glory of God in the face of Jesus Christ.

John 1:1, 4 KJV

In the beginning was the Word, and the Word was with God, and the Word was God... In him was life; and the life was the light of men.

1 John 1:7 KJV

But if we walk in the light, as he is in the light, we have fellowship one with another.

The first thing I do when I walk into the room is turn off the overhead light and switch on the smaller side lamp. The ceiling light has multiple bulbs and they all glare relentlessly, their flat and pitiless illumination carving up the room into "exposed" and "dark".

Then I light the fire in the open hearth. A dead branch (this is treasure!) has fallen from the old ash tree and we have broken it up for kindling. Wood that has died on the tree and been held in the air to season until it falls is just the best for starting a fire. The twigs we have harvested for kindling are thickly encrusted with oakmoss that burns with such a sweet fragrance.

We have some birch logs in the basket of firewood, which take quickly and burn bright. In no time at all the fire is going.

On the old Irish dresser, on the mantel shelf, on the hearth stone, I light short beeswax candles, and a tall one made from wax dyed many colours, perfumed with essential oils. And now I turn off the electric light.

So we sit in silence, Jesus and me, in firelight and candlelight. Outside the last silver gleam of day is quietening to the heavier, sombre colours of evening's wing. The day comes down to peace.

And I watch his face.

I think you could never get tired of gazing at the face of Jesus. The best way to watch anyone's face, of course, is by firelight and candlelight, for these do not compete with the shining of the inner being – they let the soul-light be seen.

In the peace and silence of firelight, in a place where no fear is, the soul comes alive, and is revealed in a person's countenance.

You can look at the face of a person watching television, and see it is not the same; they are taken out of themselves, the soul no longer bedded in the socket of the living being, but displaced into the magic of the machine. And the light is blue, eery, not friendly to the spirit.

Gazing on the face of Jesus, I come home to myself. It has not been an easy day, and I reached the end of it fraught and distracted, beset by a posse of frustrations, knocked off balance, peevish and irritable.

I know what I would have done if he had not come by to spend time with me. I would have fled from my uneasy, restless mind into the prying, violent, voyeuristic world of TV drama, or gone hunting for a world to lose myself in through the labyrinthine ways of the internet, until I exhausted myself into oblivion and dropped heavy-eyed from the screen in the small hours into sleep at last.

But this is better.

You need darkness, of course, to see light. Here in forgiving firelight, candlelight, that softens the edges of life and allows what doesn't matter to sink into shadow, I start to be able to perceive the shining of his Christlight. I can only say it is like music, as clear as morning dew, as refreshing to the soul as cool well water, as fragrant as roses in the dusk.

How would I describe the face of Jesus: peaceful and serious, composed, quietly intent? He isn't smiling right now and yet his face is full of smile. The kindness... the understanding... to draw near to him and gaze upon his face is the greatest privilege human life affords. The passing years have left my mind worn out and cynical, always wary, habitually guilty and defensive; often tired, never at rest. It is with a sense of wonder that I feel the old, sour dregs of disillusionment bathed free, until I am left only with knowing that I *adore* Jesus... his company is the dearest sweetness, the balm of my heart... letting me start again.

If time and circumstances ever give you the chance to light a fire on an open hearth, to light a candle or two, and as the night wings fold around the earth to sit down with Jesus and gaze upon his face, oh don't let that chance pass you by. It can heal your soul to the roots. It can change everything.

Day 32

Saturday of Week 5

Matthew 4:5–7 GNT

Then the Devil took Jesus to Jerusalem, the Holy City, set him on the highest point of the Temple, and said to him, "If you are God's Son, throw yourself down, for the scripture says,

'God will give orders to his angels about you;
they will hold you up with their hands,
so that not even your feet will be hurt on the stones.'"

Jesus answered, "But the scripture also says, 'Do not put the Lord your God to the test.'"

Psalm 91:14–16 NIV

"Because he loves me," says the Lord, "I will rescue him; I will protect him, for he acknowledges my name. He will call on me, and I will answer him; I will be with him in trouble, I will deliver him and honour him. With long life I will satisfy him and show him my salvation."

Isaiah 43:1–2 NRSV

Do not fear, for I have redeemed you; I have called you by name, you are mine.
When you pass through the waters, I will be with you; and through the rivers, they shall not overwhelm you; when you walk through fire you shall not be burned, and the flame shall not consume you.

Isaiah 46:3–4 (paraphrased Wilcock)

From the day of your birth I have carried you, even from before you were born. I will still be the same in your old age. When your hair is grey, you can still depend on me; I was the one who made you, I will bear you up and be your salvation.

Matthew 27:45–46 NIV

From noon until three in the afternoon darkness came over all the land. About three in the afternoon Jesus cried out in a loud voice, "Eloi, Eloi, lema sabachthani?" (which means "My God, my God, why have you forsaken me?").

"What were you getting ready for," I ask him, "when you headed off into the wilderness? Healing? Preaching? Popularity – leadership? What did you have in mind?"

He turns his head and grins at me. Softly he sings, "*There may be trouble ahead…*"

Seriously? Irving Berlin? Doesn't Jesus stick to hymns and psalms? "*Let's face the music and dance*"? I meet his gaze.

Sometimes, I do wonder at Jesus. Maybe two thousand years after the event I too would be capable of cracking a joke about all that followed his forty days in the wilderness – but even with such a time lapse… I don't know.

It occurs to me, his whole life is like a parable about trust – demonstrating what it means to trust absolutely, no questions asked.

He starts his public ministry at thirty years old, no mere lad. So many times already he must have prayed the psalms, immersed himself in those expressions of faith – "For he will command his angels concerning you to guard you in all your ways; they will lift you up in their hands, so that you will not strike your foot against a stone…" (Psalm 91:11–12). The God who is on his people's side, who goes ahead of them in battle, wipes out the enemy, delivers all the spoils of victory into the hands of his faithful. In the religion Jesus grew up with, faith and success, prosperity, are synonymous. So, how does he know? How does he know God is doing something different now, moving us on into something deeper – from justice into mercy and compassion?

Endlessly in their pilgrimage God's people cry out to their Lord to save, help, provide for them. Here's Jesus on the pinnacle of the Temple, tempted to do the same; but he doesn't need to. Because he already trusts the Father. He already sees and understands what the Father is doing. The authority of faith is rooted in his soul; he doesn't need the miracle.

He walks with God through what comes next: the crowd's adulation, and their treachery; his followers' human frailty, addiction to bickering and one-upmanship; the interminable sly baiting of the scribes and Pharisees; the insatiable needs of the poor, maimed, outcast, abandoned, lepers, blind, helpless… Amid the shoving throng wanting to gobble him down whole, the Father keeps him steady; he is not overwhelmed.

What sends a chill down my spine is the frankness of that anguished cry – *My God, my God, why have you forsaken me?* It is of all prayers the most revealing, for it looks God straight in the eye; it holds God to account as Father. And, this is no separation. God does not, as many have said, look away. On the contrary. This is the moment of becoming the Father's will, the surrendering of all self-interest and separation. This is not about God (not) saving Jesus. It's about God in Jesus saving us. How curious that being entirely subsumed into love can be experienced as abandonment – for such it is; the leaving behind forever of the little self.

There are many comfortable (and uncomfortable too, of course) things about being in the presence of Jesus; one of the best is never really having to explain. He understands. Already, he has searched me and known me. As I think through all this now, in the company of his silence, I feel the warmth of his understanding. I realize that the power of God is not to rescue us *from* our circumstances, but to keep us safe *within* all that happens to us – as the letter to the Ephesians puts it a few years down the line, "having done all, to stand".

To get ready for so deep a level of trust – complete abandonment – could only be done in wilderness; civilization has too many props.

Day 33

Passion Sunday

Isaiah 53:1–9 GNT

"Who would have believed what we now report?
Who could have seen the Lord's hand in this?
It was the will of the Lord that his servant grow like a plant
    taking root in dry ground.
He had no dignity or beauty to make us take notice of him.
There was nothing attractive about him, nothing that would
    draw us to him.
We despised him and rejected him; he endured suffering
    and pain.
No one would even look at him – we ignored him as if
    he were nothing.

"But he endured the suffering that should have been ours,
    the pain that we should have borne.
All the while we thought that his suffering was punishment
    sent by God.
But because of our sins he was wounded, beaten because of
    the evil we did.
We are healed by the punishment he suffered, made whole by
    the blows he received.
All of us were like sheep that were lost, each of us going his
    own way.
But the Lord made the punishment fall on him, the punishment
    all of us deserved.

*"He was treated harshly, but endured it humbly; he never said
     a word.*

*Like a lamb about to be slaughtered, like a sheep about to
     be sheared, he never said a word.*

*He was arrested and sentenced and led off to die, and no one
     cared about his fate.*

He was put to death for the sins of our people.

*He was placed in a grave with those who are evil, he was buried
     with the rich, even though he had never committed a crime
     or ever told a lie."*

Mark 1:12–13 GNT

*At once the Spirit made him go into the desert, where he stayed
forty days, being tempted by Satan. Wild animals were there
also, but angels came and helped him.*

Wilderness holds many contradictions; it attracts me and repels
me at the same time. It fascinates me and it scares me. I think
wilderness might be a place that makes a person grow up fast.
On the one hand I am drawn to its grandeur and beauty, its
magnificence and peace. It preserves the holistic pattern of
the earth from the predations of our ignorance – wilderness
safeguards the balance that we have a habit of destroying. We
need wilderness – without it, the earth would perish. So that's on
the plus side.

But I draw back in fear from wilderness because of its main
simple obvious characteristic: danger. Or perhaps I should say
DANGER!! (Read that in red.) Everywhere in the wilderness
I see danger: from wild animals and the harsh environment –
poisonous plants, insects, and reptiles; exposure to sun, wind,
and extreme cold; diseases both airborne and waterborne. The
danger of dying from thirst in the desert. And apart from danger,
the discouragement of being alone in the desert – it could even

drive you mad. The lack of help, too, for the solitary pilgrim in the wilderness; being too weak, small, and unskilled to adapt the environment to meet human need.

I think of Jesus, alone in the wilderness. Is he discouraged, that dauntless spirit? Does he sit listening in the dark, for the slithering of a snake or the prowling of a mountain lion? Then I see things in a different light. Oddly, for Jesus as for many others before and since, the wilderness represents a *refuge* from danger. I think of Temple officials out to get him, of the crowd shouting boisterously for him to be crucified, of Pilate's indifference and the impersonal efficiency of Roman soldiers laying on the lash, hammering in the nails. I recall times in the gospel story when his kinsmen and countrymen picked up rocks to stone him to death.

When the human social environment goes toxic and a person becomes a scapegoat for retribution, the rotten fabric of a broken justice system no longer bears the weight of the life entrusted to it. Punitive application of religious codes morph whole body politic into a system of oppression where lives are tossed aside and individuals have very little power or choice. Then the wilderness takes on the cast of a friend, a place of safety where a person has a chance. The forces of nature proceed from God and flow with the purposes of his heart, so they are never malign unless we make them so. A fox is dangerous to a chicken, but it doesn't hate the chicken. A sated lion will pass a grazing antelope in peace. Animals will kill, and sometimes play with their prey to hone their hunting skills; but no animal ever imprisoned and tortured another being for his faith, for jealousy at his righteousness, for the threat posed by his holiness in a system that stinks. The wilderness holds many terrors, but not the least of them is its natural purity. Untamed, it is less malleable than corruption.

He knows my thoughts, but still I feel impelled to ask him, "Jesus – where was wilderness really, in your life?"

I wait for his answer, and at last he says, "Wilderness is an opinion, and orientation. I carry wilderness in the same location as home: in my heart. The starry sky, the blooming after rain of ground long arid, the cry of a wolf from a high rock – only in my heart do these occur as wonder. The agony of rejection, the pain of exclusion, the dread of the mob closing in and what must follow – where are these real but in my heart?"

He pauses, and again I wait. What he says when he finally speaks, humble and low, is worth my patience.

"The thing is, I have brought the wilderness home. Whose heart lodges safe in my heart finds shelter from exile, and all fear of the storm dissolves. In me you can find peace, because I have overcome the world."

Day 34

Monday of Week 6

Philippians 4:4 NRSV

Rejoice in the Lord always; again I will say, Rejoice.

2 Corinthians 9:7 KJV

Every man according as he purposeth in his heart, so let him give; not grudgingly, or of necessity: for God loveth a cheerful giver.

Matthew 6:16–18 NIV

"When you fast, do not look sombre as the hypocrites do, for they disfigure their faces to show others they are fasting. Truly I tell you, they have received their reward in full. But when you fast, put oil on your head and wash your face, so that it will not be obvious to others that you are fasting, but only to your Father, who is unseen; and your Father, who sees what is done in secret, will reward you."

Matthew 5:43–48 GNT

"You have heard that it was said, 'Love your friends, hate your enemies.' But now I tell you: love your enemies and pray for those who persecute you, so that you may become the children of your Father in heaven. For he makes his sun to shine on bad and good people alike, and gives rain to those who do good and to those who do evil. Why should God reward you if you love only the people who love you? Even the tax collectors do that! And if

you speak only to your friends, have you done anything out of the ordinary? Even the pagans do that! You must be perfect – just as your Father in heaven is perfect."

"The way I see it is, there's no point in trying to look cheerful; you know what's in my heart anyway. Why bother?"

Jesus says nothing to this, but – well, flawless logic, innit?

I push my hands deeper into my pockets and wish I'd remembered my gloves. Or I wish I lived in Florida. Or Australia. California would be nice. Anywhere warmer than England with the wind blowing strong from the east, on the coast in the middle of March. You can't beat this cold drear for misery.

This has been a bad week. Muddle and miscommunication. Things taking forever to do that should have been easy. I feel snarky and out of sorts. So we walk along, and I can't help noticing the silence of Jesus sounds particularly loud.

"What?" I stop and look at him. "What?" He looks back.

"One of the most underrated and beautiful disciplines in the kingdom of heaven," he says, "is cheerfulness." This comment he makes with a little grin, kind of half apologetic.

"Oh, thanks!" I snap at him. "That's just what I need to hear."

I know this anyway. Of course I do. I know that happiness is not something that happens to you, it's something you choose and practise, deliberately. I know happiness is not a destination, a distant goal – it's the path you travel, the way of walking, the direction of the journey that means the destination takes care of itself. I know how good those people make me feel who always have a smile and a kind word, find something encouraging and friendly to say every time. I know that cheerfulness is a facet of forgiveness sometimes – a gentle touch of love smoothing over misunderstandings and altercations of the past. It's just, today I'm not in the mood.

Of course the whole point of any kind of discipline is exactly that – doing it when you're not in the mood. If you're only kind and friendly when things are going well, what's the use of that? If you're only nice to the people you like and cold-shoulder everybody else, how does that build the kingdom? I know that perfectly well.

But sometimes a person just needs some space. Sometimes you don't feel ready for any kind of interaction. Sometimes you're just plain grumpy and that's how it is and it takes a little while to come round from it – and what's wrong with that? Can't I just tell it like it is from time to time?

I hunch deeper into my coat, glowering at the greyness of the day. I feel backed into a corner and resentful. *One of the most underrated and beautiful disciplines in the kingdom of heaven is cheerfulness.* Oh, thanks!

We have covered about half a mile while all this churns around in my gut and ties itself in knots in my head. I feel completely hopeless now, despondent and belligerent. All this while, Jesus says nothing. He just goes on walking beside me.

And eventually it dawns on me, this is really stupid. How to squander an opportunity, how to waste a morning!

I realize that every moment is a choice, each passing minute offers a doorway to who I could be. Turning a whole day around is just one step away.

So I stop. He stops. I turn to look at him. I take a deep breath.

"I'm sorry," I say.

He grins at me and gives me a hug.

Jesus hugs me.

Imagine that.

Tuesday of Week 6

Philippians 4:5 RSV

Let all men know your forbearance. The Lord is at hand.

1 Corinthians 13:4–5 NRSV

Love is patient; love is kind; love is not envious or boastful or arrogant or rude. It does not insist on its own way; it is not irritable or resentful...

Mark 9:36–37 NRSV

Then he took a little child and put it among them; and taking it in his arms, he said to them, "Whoever welcomes one such child in my name welcomes me, and whoever welcomes me welcomes not me but the one who sent me."

Now, the thing I had forgotten about the four o'clock is that it is the conveyance of choice for the school children. It's why I usually take the five-twenty-three instead. A sense of gloom descends on me as we approach the bus stop. The regular rabble is there.

For the next ten minutes we wait in a silence broken all too penetratingly by the *fortissimo possibile* observations of one particularly obnoxious child bent on discussing dead bodies, deformities, and details I would have preferred never to have considered about conjoined twins.

When the bus (finally) arrives, without consulting Jesus

I swing into the very front seat just behind the driver's cab, knowing I can rely on the school children heading with equal determination for the long bench seat at the very back of the bus. Though it is a long vehicle and full of passengers, not a syllable is lost to me of the continuing babble of this schoolchild, who has now moved on to taunting his associates, asking persistent questions, and discussing sweets.

As usual when travelling home on this service, I run and re-run scenarios in my head fantasizing a variety of confrontations with this unattractive juvenile, requiring him to either turn down the volume or temper the content of his discourse.

Jesus did once say that unless we change and become like little children, we shall never enter the kingdom of heaven. I wonder if he might feel ready to reconsider.

Our young scholar's stop is reached halfway home, and I am inexpressibly grateful to see him depart (without a word of thanks to the bus driver).

As the bus shudders and lurches its way through these country lanes, we pass the small stone chapel among the trees down by the river. The sight of it brings back to my mind a recent conversation with a friend, who remarked on a mutual acquaintance having transferred allegiance to this little church, having been driven out along with large numbers of the flock, from the big church in the high street, because of the objectionable and insensitively expressed views of the new rector. Our friend is a mild and easy-going man, but the rector's approach to life and faith is so offensively and unrelentingly aggressive that not even the most genial temperament could remain unruffled. I have met the cleric in question myself, but would not willingly offer to repeat the experience.

I wonder what Jesus would have to say about this. I wonder what his own reactions would be. I wonder how he thinks it would be right to respond to this frightful child, and the appalling clergyman. When I say "I wonder", I don't intend to ask him because I'm not sure I actually want to know. Some questions can make life very awkward when brought forth from dormancy into active mode.

We roll through the traffic lights into Silverhill. Jesus rings the bell (I think he likes doing this; they didn't have them in first-century Galilee) and the bus draws up alongside the chip shop near the corner of our road.

As we walk along past the carpet warehouse and the doctor's surgery, Jesus says, "It's the same thing in both cases, really."

There is something unsettling about a companion who can completely read your mind. I know there's no point in pretending I don't know what he's talking about, so "Go on," I say.

"Well… first off you have to get past the crossroads where you decide if you're going to love them or not. That has to be a given. So long as the jury's out on whether to love someone at all or not, how can you possibly progress to figuring out *how* to love them? If case by case, person by person, you have to decide if this one is worth loving, you will never begin. So you have to begin by putting in place the assumption that they are all worth loving – not only by the Father but by you. And not only as a hypothesis but as a plan of action.

"After that, having moved on from 'can I?' to 'how can I?' the trick is to lift up the cover and peek underneath. Your friend's pastor is uncompromising, obdurate, and rigid – and does that not smell of fear? What casts out fear but love? Love that believes in a person and hopes for them, takes joy in them – finds them delightful. What's needed is the unreasoning unconditional devotion of a mother for her small child.

"It's the same with the schoolboy – underneath the rather unsophisticated facade of noisy braggadocio and exhibitionism is something desperately unsure of itself, someone so unconfident they believe a trumpet blast must be necessary to secure them attention, rescue them from the terror of anonymity and obscurity.

"Reassurance will heal what hostility can only exacerbate."

I change the subject as we walk up our path, offering him a cup of tea – which he sounds pleased to accept. Uneasily, I wonder if he is really pleased, or if I am on a long list of people he firmly decided to love. Either way, there is something very peaceful in the company of someone whose loving-kindness is just a given; someone who accepts you without question, so you can just be yourself, without all the contortions of winning their approval.

Day 36

Wednesday of Week 6

Matthew 17:1–2 GNT

Six days later Jesus took with him Peter and the brothers James and John and led them up a high mountain where they were alone. As they looked on, a change came over Jesus: his face was shining like the sun, and his clothes were dazzling white.

John 20:14–16 GNT

Then she turned around and saw Jesus standing there; but she did not know that it was Jesus. "Woman, why are you crying?" Jesus asked her. "Who is it that you are looking for?"

She thought he was the gardener, so she said to him, "If you took him away, sir, tell me where you have put him, and I will go and get him."

Jesus said to her, "Mary!"

1 Corinthians 13:12 NRSV

For now we see in a mirror, dimly, but then we will see face to face. Now I know only in part; then I will know fully, even as I have been fully known.

1 John 3:2 GNT

My dear friends, we are now God's children, but it is not yet clear what we shall become. But we know that when Christ appears, we shall be like him, because we shall see him as he really is.

I asked him to come with me into this particular wilderness because it felt so daunting.

My friend's husband had died, and she was angry and distraught, in despair really. It's not so much that I thought she'd have a go at me – she's way too nice for that – more that I felt scared of hurting her even more by insensitivity or pushing my own views. But at the same time I thought that if only I could share with her some of the hope and the comfort and healing I have found keeping company with Jesus, it might be a lifeline for her in all the bewilderness of pain and grief and loss.

So I asked him to come with me, and he did.

We came into her house together and sat side by side on her sofa, and at first I thought she was just absorbed in the introversion of deep emotion and not really paying attention, but gradually it dawned on me – she couldn't see him. There he was, sitting right next to me, quietly, peacefully listening – and she couldn't see him at all! Had no idea he was there!

He made a difference. Some of her rage eased a little, and made space for the sorrow to be expressed. We were able to talk through a few of the practical things she felt afraid of. Most of all she just told me about the memories – his illness, the excruciating journey of his dying, how helpless she had felt and how inadequate. She remembered back to their early days, to some of the best times – the travelling, the music, the animals, the freedom, the fun. So I mainly just listened for a couple of hours, and when we left she smiled and gave me a hug and said it had helped. But still she couldn't see him, nor did she notice when he put out his hand and ever so gently touched her cheek as we made our farewells.

"What's with that?" I ask him as we thread our way home through the footpaths that criss-cross the town. "How come I can see you and she can't?"

He looks at me and grins. "You can't see me either."

And now I'm completely baffled. "Yes..." I hesitate, confused. "Yes I can. What d'you mean?"

I stand still where I am, staring at him, puzzled. He's laughing at me – not unkind, full of fun, affectionate, loving, his brown eyes shining. Of course I can see him: this is Jesus, just how I always imagined him, his homespun robe a bit scruffy, his beard and tumbling black hair reaching past shoulder length, his hands so expressive, with the scars at the wrists, his sandals – Jesus. Everyone knows what Jesus looks like. "Well?" I demand an explanation.

"Well..." he begins, "what you see when you look at me is partly what I am and partly just how you think of me. There was a time, high on a mountain, when friends of mine were taken by surprise to see me as I really am, and it knocked them silly for a minute or two. If you saw me as I am, it would hurt your eyes, and what would be the point of that? So I let you see what you're expecting; and that's how you know it's me. That might change, over time. You might come to see me differently. But if you do, that won't be because I've changed, it'll be because you've changed. Your friend – just now all she can see is herself, because her grief is so big. That happened to a friend of mine, too, after... when she had lost me. I came to find her but she couldn't see me properly – didn't recognize me – because all she could see was her grief. It's okay. It's still me. I'm still here."

"Oh."

This feels a bit disconcerting. I mean, I know we have never really been able to determine how much of what we see happens out there and how much inside our own heads – is the colour green in the grass or in the wiring of our brains? Even so... suddenly Jesus seems that bit less real.

"I am really here," he reassures me, understanding what's going through my mind, "even when you can't see me, can't feel me – like your friend couldn't. I'm still here. I am always with you. And one day – I promise you – you will see me as I really am."

Day 37

Thursday of Week 6

Luke 7:36–44 NIV

When one of the Pharisees invited Jesus to have dinner with him, he went to the Pharisee's house and reclined at the table. A woman in that town who lived a sinful life learned that Jesus was eating at the Pharisee's house, so she came there with an alabaster jar of perfume. As she stood behind him at his feet weeping, she began to wet his feet with her tears. Then she wiped them with her hair, kissed them and poured perfume on them.

When the Pharisee who had invited him saw this, he said to himself, "If this man were a prophet, he would know who is touching him and what kind of woman she is – that she is a sinner."

Jesus answered him, "Simon, I have something to tell you."

"Tell me, teacher," he said.

"Two people owed money to a certain money-lender. One owed him five hundred denarii, and the other fifty. Neither of them had the money to pay him back, so he forgave the debts of both. Now which of them will love him more?"

Simon replied, "I suppose the one who had the bigger debt forgiven."

"You have judged correctly," Jesus said.

Then he turned towards the woman and said to Simon, "Do you see this woman?"

You can believe this or not: I am invisible. This is no idle claim. I should have been a spy. I can pass within a foot of someone

I've known since forever and they will not notice me. I can stand in a shop alongside a friend of twenty years' acquaintance, and they will not see me. Even members of my own family searching for me in a crowd look straight at me and do not see me. I am uncommonly forgettable. I have nothing about me to draw your attention or fix me in your mind. This doesn't upset me, it's very convenient – and a handy attribute for a writer. People will say all kinds of things in my presence they might have more cautiously kept to themselves if they'd registered I was there. I am the definitive nobody.

I think more people might be invisible if they weren't recognized by their identifying label. Like those grand social occasions where the arriving guests give their card to the butler and he announces, "The Duchess of Cornwall" or "The Akond of Swat" or whoever it is. Knowing what people are can easily be confused for knowing who they are: "Oh yes, I know him – he's the butcher. Sure I know her – she's the receptionist from the surgery."

One of my all-time favourite stories from the Gospels is that one where Jesus goes to dinner with Simon. A story of who and what. Simon may or may not know Jesus personally – I suspect that he wants Jesus at his dinner party because by this time Jesus has become a personality, a public figure, the Preacher from Galilee. Simon himself has the odd distinction of two identifying features from opposite ends of the spectrum – the Pharisee (respected religious elite) and the Leper (social outcast). I make a mental note to ask Jesus, "Was this man one of those you healed?"

And when the uninvited woman gatecrashes the party and begins her uninhibited adoration, I don't know what the Leper thinks but the Pharisee is appalled. If you were a Prophet (he thinks as he looks at the scene), you would know this woman is a Sinner. Categories writ large!

What I love is the way Jesus completely ignores every single category in his question, "Simon; do you see this woman?" He sees the person, not the label.

As this day comes to a close, I think back on the time I spent with Jesus as we wandered together through the concrete wilderness of our shopping centre with its chain stores and cheap mass-produced garments and gadgets. We were people-watching, and I loved hearing his comments – he saw that the child in the stroller was crying because her fingers were cold, that the old lady in the bus queue was looking longingly at the occupied seats in the shelter, her feet swollen and tired. He heard the defeat and defensiveness in the voice of the young man arguing with his girlfriend; he noticed the cheerful expression on the face of the man who sweeps up the rubbish in the shopping mall. He didn't have to be told what they were to understand who they were.

Something I notice about Jesus is that he is not frightened by anger or repulsed by aggression and swagger. He is not vulnerable to manipulation or flattery. He looks, and he really sees – the motivation, the intention, and sometimes the underlying reality that even the person he's looking at cannot find because it is too deeply buried under layers of accumulated life.

"Jesus," I say, closing my eyes, remembering, holding his presence in my heart as though he is still really there, "teach me to see as you see. Teach me to see beyond the facades and the status, beyond my own prejudice and in spite of my assumptions. Teach me to see like you."

The darkness is folded all around me, and I am alone here in my bedroom. Even so, I know his voice in my heart; I could never mistake it. "I will teach you," he says.

Friday of Week 6

Luke 21:34–38 GNT

"Be careful not to let yourselves become occupied with too much feasting and drinking and with the worries of this life, or that Day may suddenly catch you like a trap. For it will come upon all people everywhere on earth. Be on watch and pray always that you will have the strength to go safely through all those things that will happen and to stand before the Son of Man."

Jesus spent those days teaching in the Temple, and when evening came, he would go out and spend the night on the Mount of Olives. Early each morning all the people went to the Temple to listen to him.

John 8:1–11 GNT

Then everyone went home, but Jesus went to the Mount of Olives. Early the next morning he went back to the Temple. All the people gathered around him, and he sat down and began to teach them. The teachers of the Law and the Pharisees brought in a woman who had been caught committing adultery, and they made her stand before them all. "Teacher," they said to Jesus, "this woman was caught in the very act of committing adultery. In our Law Moses commanded that such a woman must be stoned to death. Now, what do you say?" They said this to trap Jesus, so that they could accuse him. But he bent over and wrote on the ground with his finger. As they stood there asking him questions, he straightened up and said to them, "Whichever one of you has committed no sin may throw the first stone at her." Then he bent over again and wrote on the ground. When they heard this, they all left, one by one, the older ones first. Jesus was left alone, with the woman still standing there. He straightened up and said to her, "Where are they? Is there no one left to condemn you?"

"No one, sir," she answered.

"Well, then," Jesus said, "I do not condemn you either. Go, but do not sin again."

John 6:15 GNT

Jesus knew that they were about to come and seize him in order to make him king by force; so he went off again to the hills by himself.

I love the night wind. Its fragrance is peaceful and its quietness stirs with life. The night feels alert and vital to me as I lie in the darkness, listening to a fox bark across the valley and breathing the cool air.

Outside my window a yellow streetlight shines relentlessly, so my heavy linen curtains close out the stars. Behind them, just alongside my bed, the window is open to let me feel the night, so I am not cut off from its urgent pulsing mystery.

In Galilee, mountains run the whole length of the country, and the desert can be just a few minutes away from the fertile lands. Rocky hilltops, green valleys, and the silvery green of the olive groves cladding the terraced hills make a patchwork of the landscape. The Sea of Galilee is cradled between the Golan Heights and the Galilean hills.

It's colder at night up in the hills. The evening breeze would have been welcome after the hot, dry heat of the day. But there is even snow sometimes high in the mountains.

"Did you light a little fire, Jesus, for the comfort of warmth in the hours of darkness?"

I try to picture him there, seeking the peace of solitude, taking refuge in the vast silence of the Father's presence, love like a rock to lean on.

Like an African elephant sucking up water, fifteen litres at one go; like a huge tanker filling up with thirty tons of life-saving water to take to a place of drought; like a camel slaking its thirst, sucking in twenty gallons of water ready for the long trip across the desert – that ancient soul, the great and noble soul of Jesus drinking, drinking, drinking in the Father's love and power, in the loneliness of the Mount of Olives, in the peaceful silence of night.

In those night hours alone with the Father, he incubated the wisdom and love, the strength of purpose, to speak truth to power and lift up the fallen in all that the day would bring.

"But Jesus," I whisper, "Jesus… were you never afraid all alone in the mountains at night?"

The silence speaks, and I know his answer. There is nothing in nature to frighten Jesus, no wild beast, no living thing at all, that does not recognize his authority and worship him. Only the evil lodged like an alien glass splinter in the human heart. There was a night in Gethsemane when the fear of what was to come almost broke him, and then he was lonely indeed. But apart from that, there is no loneliness in the heart of Jesus; the hills and the wild goats, the timid conies and the fierce lions, the tossing storms and screaming wind, they find themselves at home in his presence – they are at peace. Jesus has entered into the heart of night and drawn the sting of its desolation, because he is the light of the world.

"Jesus," I tell him, "Jesus… I love the night… I love the reassurance of your presence intensified here in the darkness."

Knowing he is with me, taking refuge in the silence of his presence, love like a rock to lean on, my eyes close in peace.

Day 39

Saturday of Week 6

Luke 10:38–42 NIV

As Jesus and his disciples were on their way, he came to a village where a woman named Martha opened her home to him. She had a sister called Mary, who sat at the Lord's feet listening to what he said. But Martha was distracted by all the preparations that had to be made. She came to him and asked, "Lord, don't you care that my sister has left me to do the work by myself? Tell her to help me!"

"Martha, Martha," the Lord answered, "you are worried and upset about many things, but few things are needed – or indeed only one. Mary has chosen what is better, and it will not be taken away from her."

Matthew 6:31–33 NIV

So do not worry, saying, "What shall we eat?" or "What shall we drink?" or "What shall we wear?" For the pagans run after all these things, and your heavenly Father knows that you need them. But seek first his kingdom and his righteousness, and all these things will be given to you as well.

I can hardly believe that I am going to admit this publicly, but I kind of hoped Jesus wouldn't show up today – only because I've been soooooo busy. Lying in bed this morning, mentally reviewing the day, for the first time it began to feel like… like his visits can be a bit of a nuisance sometimes?

What are you thinking? Where is an interrobang (‽) when you need one? I was shocked at myself. I mean – well – *Jesus!* What a privilege – to spend time with *Jesus!* Wouldn't that always be more important than anyone else? I think it's quite brave of me to own up.

So much to remember. So much on my mind. So many things to juggle. So much to get done.

But I make time for him (big of me, eh?) when he comes by just after I've snatched a hasty lunch. He wants us to go down by the sea, because it's a beautiful day and the sun's shining, but I haven't got time to walk all the way there and all the way back *and* sit by the sea – so we compromise and take a bus. I know. There are no buses in the wilderness. Okay, but you do have to get there somehow.

So here we are sitting together in the lee of the wall that holds up the foreshore promenade. Sheltered from the wind it's surprisingly warm. Jesus says nothing for a while. I look at the beach pebbles. I gaze out across the sea, sparkling with myriad points of light. I tip my head back to let my eyes feast on clouds, impossibly white against a sky indescribably blue. I listen to the quiet deep voice of the sea as the waves fall, and the drag of the shingle as they recede. I breathe in the briny purity of the air. It feels good. I begin to relax.

Not much time passes before I begin to worry about things awaiting my attention at home. I haven't got a watch. Jesus hasn't either. I throw an agitated glance at him, beginning to fret.

"Martha must have felt like I do today," I say ruefully, "at Bethany. With so many things to do."

I pause. "Maybe I should cut down a bit."

He still says nothing, so I glance his way again. "D'you think I should prune out a few commitments?"

Sometimes you do have to wait before Jesus speaks. But he does say something eventually.

"It's…" He stops again. "It's not about how many," he says, hesitantly, as if he can't quite put this into words.

"In every life…" (I wait patiently) "… there is a great deal going on within and around you. The temptation is always to become distracted. Martha was distracted by the many things. The concerns clamour – 'What shall I eat, what shall I wear, how will I pay these bills?' The questions remain, the tasks must be done… but… if you can only take a step back from them, and give yourself permission to breathe, to just be. Otherwise you lose yourself in all the things… you start to identify with them, they each carry away a little part of you. If even for a few moments you can stop, and be still – just know 'I am'; not I am this or I am that, but know the I Am that you find inside."

He stops speaking for a moment, and his gaze – steady, pure, peaceful as the sky – rests on the beauty of the ocean.

"All the things claim your attention – that's the problem," he says then. "They seem to matter so much. But when you give them your attention, they do not resolve, they grow and proliferate. It's not a matter of quantity but of focus. The kingdom of heaven is like a merchant looking for pearls. Then he came upon one of such beauty, such worth, he gave up everything he had to make it his. He left behind the many – d'you see? – to gain the one.

"Each thought, each preoccupation and task, seems so important. They clamour. This is true of feelings, too. Martha – yes, she had so much to think about. And soon she had irritation and resentment and frustration to think about too. She was run ragged by everything going on inside and around her. It took her over.

"Trying to reschedule, cut down, prune out – well, that might be sensible, there are only twenty-four hours in each day. But then rescheduling becomes another thing to do – the simplifying turns into a complicated game. Yes, there are things to be done – as the bird builds a nest, as the wood ant carries a tiny splinter back to the citadel, so do men and women fulfil their human destiny. But underneath it all, only one thing matters; if you become distracted from that you have – literally – lost your life. If you can keep your focus on the one thing, then all the rest will fall into place. I mean the mystery of the presence of God within your heart."

Silence expands around us. The waves keep their peaceful interminable rhythm, like a heartbeat of life.

Day 40

Palm Sunday

John 9:13–16 NRSV

They brought to the Pharisees the man who had formerly been blind. Now it was a sabbath day when Jesus made the mud and opened his eyes. Then the Pharisees also began to ask him how he had received his sight. He said to them, "He put mud on my eyes. Then I washed, and now I see." Some of the Pharisees said, "This man is not from God, for he does not observe the sabbath."

Matthew 26:57–68 NRSV

Those who had arrested Jesus took him to Caiaphas the high priest, in whose house the scribes and the elders had gathered. But Peter was following him at a distance, as far as the courtyard of the high priest; and going inside, he sat with the guards in order to see how this would end. Now the chief priests and the whole council were looking for false testimony against Jesus so that they might put him to death, but they found none, though many false witnesses came forward. At last two came forward and said, "This fellow said, 'I am able to destroy the temple of God and to build it in three days.'" The high priest stood up and said, "Have you no answer? What is it that they testify against you?" But Jesus was silent. Then the high priest said to him, "I put you under oath before the living God, tell us if you are the Messiah, the Son of God." Jesus said to him,

"You have said so. But I tell you,

From now on you will see the Son of Man seated at the right hand of Power and coming on the clouds of heaven."

Then the high priest tore his clothes and said, "He has blasphemed! Why do we still need witnesses? You have now heard his blasphemy. What is your verdict?" They answered, "He deserves death." Then they spat in his face and struck him; and some slapped him, saying, "Prophesy to us, you Messiah! Who is it that struck you?"

After church, we walk up over the hill, then along to the corner shop to buy some croissants – hot croissants and a pot of coffee are what this day with its razor-sharp east wind needs! I must confess I feel a bit embarrassed suggesting Sunday shopping to Jesus, of all people; but he doesn't seem overly bothered.

Then it's just across the road and through the valley via the park, home to put the oven on and boil a kettle. Oh, the fragrance of that coffee! Oh the crispy shell of those croissants, and their soft, doughy insides… Oh my! I will *never* make an ascetic.

Jesus sits on a kitchen stool at our table, licking butter off his fingers with that rapt absorption I like to see. Makes me happy. He's not much of an ascetic either.

So I ask him, "Why did you need to go out into the wilderness? I know in the case of most people it would be a searching for God thing – finding their true self, connecting with mystery, getting in touch with the eternal and whatnot. But surely in your case – well, I mean… you are actually that thing, aren't you? The way, the truth, and the life. What's to connect with? And, for that matter, why would I need to go into the wilderness either? Can't I just go to church?"

His eyes are brown. And they look at you in a rather penetrating way.

"It's to do with belief structures," he says.

"Explain?" I pour him some more coffee, to go with his second croissant. Jesus likes milky coffee. I'm surprised he's not fat; he likes everything!

"In the temple, in the synagogue, in the church," he says, with a kind of reluctant tone like he'd rather not be putting this into words, "there's always a Pharisee handy with a set of belief structures, with the primary purpose of making people wrong."

"Belief structures?" (My turn to lick fingers free of butter.) "Don't they matter, then? Dogma? Doctrines? Creeds? Anything goes, you mean?"

Jesus shakes his head: "Not that." He drinks his coffee, thinking. "It's more that… well, it's primarily about lived experience, don't you see? Not so much about doctrine. Not really about what you know. Or at least – it *is* about knowing, but knowing someone not something – a different kind of knowing.

"And the trouble arises when belief structures – rules, dogma, creeds – come first. If they do that, then they inhibit experience. It's meant to be the other way round. They are meant to express or explain experience, not determine it.

"When they come first, they get in the way – cramp your style. How can you be yourself with someone if you come into their presence with a manual detailing what you must say and how you must regard them, what you must conclude about them, and what you must not dare to think? How can you truly give yourself to someone in love if you are afraid of him – afraid of getting it wrong?"

He dabs around his plate with his finger, picking up the last delicious remnants of the crumbs. I watch him – his eyelashes, the tumbling hair, the soft-rough homespun undyed wool of his clothes. So very real.

"The point of wilderness is to forget all of that. It is to give you the privacy of silence and space. A place where preconceptions cease, where you reach the end of yourself. Then the Father, whose quietness is a step further down yet from silence, can make himself known. And – it will not be awful, whatever they have told you. His love is simple and kind. He loves you."

He looks up suddenly and grins at me. "Thank you," he says. "That was scrumptious!'

Day 41

Monday of Holy Week

Luke 2:27–28, 33–35 GNT

When the parents brought the child Jesus into the Temple to do
for him what the Law required, Simeon took the child in his
arms and gave thanks to God…

… The child's father and mother were amazed at the things
Simeon said about him. Simeon blessed them and said to Mary,
his mother, "This child is chosen by God for the destruction and
the salvation of many in Israel. He will be a sign from God which
many people will speak against and so reveal their secret thoughts.
And sorrow, like a sharp sword, will break your own heart."

"What?" he asks.

With anyone else I know it's better to keep my mouth shut
if I'm in a mood, for fear of saying something I may regret later.
But I have the feeling with Jesus, it's not so much that he doesn't
know the thoughts of my heart as that I don't. Until I speak them
out in his presence, actually tell him, I don't see them for what
they are. You can tell Jesus anything.

So I say, "The consecration of violence. That's what's
bothering me."

And he waits. His silence invites me, "Say more."

"Violence," I explain, "is woven into the Scriptures like a
metallic thread that catches and clings so it can't ever be separated
or drawn out. Wars and massacres, hell and damnation. This
bloodthirsty vengeful God demanding sacrifice and stonings,

commanding the putting out of eyes and running through with swords. Why weren't you born into something gentle – some religion not knee-deep in blood? Look, right from the beginning, there you are – taken by your mother to be circumcised as commanded by God. Why would God do that? Make babies as they are then command something as violent as circumcision? Do you know how violent circumcision is? You should read about it someday!"

"I know about circumcision," he says quietly.

"Then –" I'm in full flood now – "this talk of sorrow piercing your mother's heart like a sharp sword, and of you being born for people's destruction, and two thousand years of people saying what a wonderful thing it was you were crucified for their sins! What was that phrase they coined in the Middle Ages? '*O felix culpa*' – O happy sin – because it meant you would come and be crucified for us. It's not a happy sin, it's a vile black bloody awful sin that ends in so hideous and grisly a consequence. I hate it – the consecration of violence! How come it's in the Scriptures, in the church, wound tight like a tangle of barbed wire round Christianity?"

Jesus is never quick to jump in. I'm never quite sure whether I'm waiting for him to speak or he's waiting to see if I've finished – but it comes to the same thing for practical purposes. Waiting. But he gets there in the end.

"This gentle religion," he says, "what had you in mind?"

"Oh, I don't know – Buddhism, Taoism, Hinduism?"

"Well…" he speaks softly, "maybe you'd better read around a bit more – your heritage has no monopoly on violence." He pauses. "The thing is…" (I wait.)

"The thing is… what it means to be Emmanuel involves coming into life as it actually is, sharing its reality, being immersed in it. Life is violent. The antelope is brought down by the lion, the mouse snatched up in the talons of the owl, the bird taken by the night fox. And human beings hurt one another. Here and there is a brief glimpsing vision of something different – the lion and the lamb, a little child shall lead them, they shall not kill or destroy in all my holy mountain – but how to get to it?"

"Well?" I am still feeling belligerent. "Go on, then! How?"

He swallows. Am I making this difficult? I wonder.

"In each of us – each life – is the chance to realize gentleness. To build the peaceable kingdom. I never circumcised anyone. I never stoned anyone. I never crucified anyone. To the circumciser I offered myself as the baby. To angry men clutching stones I offered the challenge of searching their hearts. To the authorities with their lash and their cross I gave my body. And where was God in all this? What was God's attitude, God's stance? Dearest, don't you know who I Am?"

Mentally, I circle this, prodding it suspiciously. Is it really that simple?

There is, I know, no loyalty, courage, or compassion without adversity. Without vulnerability, there can be no meaning to kindness. The world that had never known cruelty could not understand mercy. Whichever way you look at it, life that is all comfortable can teach us nothing worth knowing. That's how it is. Maybe that's why God is called I Am, and why God is mystery. Whatever God may be, holiness is not something fanciful but is the core of reality. God is not imaginary, the projection of our dreams. God is not even "for real". It's the other way round. Reality *comes from* God. If the reality of holiness is kindness, courage, hope – where can we learn that but in the midst of this mess? Where can a star shine except the night sky?

I imagine these hands that broke bread, touched lepers, rested on the heads of little children, hammered by great four-inch forged nails into the wood of the cross. He is no namby-pamby pushover, Jesus. He spoke, and lived, fearlessly. But his way is always the same. He goes where brutality is and offers himself as gentleness – gentleness incarnate, I mean.

Right now, sitting here with me, he turns his head. There's a question, an almost-smile in his eyes.

"You can't have resurrection without death," he says, "but remember – it's done; for all time. I did it for you."

Day 42

Tuesday of Holy Week

Psalm 24:7 NRSV

Lift up your heads, O gates!
and be lifted up, O ancient doors!
that the King of glory may come in.

Isaiah 40:3–5 NRSV

A voice cries out:
"In the wilderness prepare the way of the Lord, make straight
in the desert a highway for our God.
Every valley shall be lifted up, and every mountain and hill
be made low;
the uneven ground shall become level, and the rough places
a plain.
Then the glory of the Lord shall be revealed, and all people
shall see it together, for the mouth of the Lord has spoken."

Matthew 3:1–3 NRSV

In those days John the Baptist appeared in the wilderness of
Judea, proclaiming, "Repent, for the kingdom of heaven has
come near." This is the one of whom the prophet Isaiah spoke
when he said,
"The voice of one crying out in the wilderness:
'Prepare the way of the Lord, make his paths straight.'"

Matthew 11:7–10 NRSV

*As they went away, Jesus began to speak to the crowds about
John: "What did you go out into the wilderness to look at?
A reed shaken by the wind? What then did you go out to see?
Someone dressed in soft robes? Look, those who wear soft robes
are in royal palaces. What then did you go out to see? A prophet?
Yes, I tell you, and more than a prophet. This is the one about
whom it is written,*

*'See, I am sending my messenger ahead of you,
who will prepare your way before you.'"*

Not much grows in the desert, but religion certainly does. I
think about Abraham, leaving the fertile banks of the Euphrates
River and striking out in the desert, where he came so close to
God, and God came so close to him. I think of the wandering
tribes of Israel, coming up out of the desert towards Canaan,
the Promised Land, God going before them, pillar of cloud by
day, pillar of fire by night. I think of the Church Fathers, wild
monks in their desert caves, fasting and praying. And John the
Baptist, his soul inhabited entirely by the terrifying climate of the
desert, its searing heat and bone-chilling cold, its austerity and
monotony, its howling storms of whirling wind and stinging sand.

I guess it's not surprising really. The desert wilderness has
magnificence, grandeur, a terrible beauty – but it doesn't offer
much in the way of distraction. If you want a place that will
either drive you crazy or let you hear the voice of God, this has
to be it.

There's a rhythm, a breathing in and breathing out, a
heartbeat, going on. The people of God called into the desert,
into wilderness and isolation, stark simplicity, provisional,
marginal living – then sent forth to build the peaceable kingdom,
to establish order and justice, to teach and inspire, to breathe
out the living word breathed in during desert days of wandering

in company with God alone. The desert makes space for the arrival, the entrance, of the holy.

Sometimes you get it in macro – a *whole life*, like John the Baptist's, immersed in the divine presence in the desert's majestic asceticism, forming his herald soul. A whole life breathing in! The outbreath charged with the fragrance of the holy: "Behold! The Lamb of God!"

But in most lives the rhythm is there to see, as it is in the life of Jesus, by day teaching in the Temple, by night retreating to the hills; withdrawing to the desert wilderness to fast and pray, to prepare, then coming forth to teach and heal, to proclaim.

"Does everyone have to spend time in the desert, in the wilderness?" I ask him. "Do I have to? What does it mean for me? The desert frightens me. I don't want to go. I just want to stay at home."

He considers my question. He knows me, my craving for comfort and security – neither of which the desert offers as far as I'm aware!

"Do you not need peace?" he asks me gently. "Do you not need time to think and dream? Haven't there been times when you went into your room and shut the door, huddled up on your bed and pleaded with the Father, your heart torn? Haven't I seen you look up into the wideness of the sky, and whisper, 'This is what I came here to see'?"

"Is that the same?" If that's my desert it certainly lacks the harsh rigours of the places John the Baptist called home. "Is that good enough?"

He smiles. "In the dreamscape of every heart's interior country, part of the territory is desert. Every life finds itself in the boondocks at some point or other. Wilderness is necessary. You can't really make your soul without it. Some are drawn to the heights of the mountains and accept the challenge with gladness, coming down to the valley again with their faces shining. Others are pitched into the wasteland gasping, wondering whatever happened to them, and come out by dint of determined struggle to recapture what they regard as normal. But you need it. Everyone does. Without it your soul can't grow up."

"Like a Christmas cactus that can't flower without passing through a cold spell," I muse. "Like a bear hibernating through the winter high in its mountain cave, then emerging in the spring to nibble on fern shoots and come back down to the valley to catch fish and start eating again. Like a fire salamander emerging from its larval stage in water, crawling up out of it onto dry land, to become what it was meant to be."

"Yes," says Jesus. "Something like that."

Day 43

Wednesday of Holy Week

John 17:15–23 GNT

I do not ask you to take them out of the world, but I do ask you to keep them safe from the Evil One. Just as I do not belong to the world, they do not belong to the world. Dedicate them to yourself by means of the truth; your word is truth. I sent them into the world, just as you sent me into the world. And for their sake I dedicate myself to you, in order that they, too, may be truly dedicated to you.

"I pray not only for them, but also for those who believe in me because of their message. I pray that they may all be one. Father! May they be in us, just as you are in me and I am in you. May they be one, so that the world will believe that you sent me. I gave them the same glory you gave me, so that they may be one, just as you and I are one: I in them and you in me, so that they may be completely one, in order that the world may know that you sent me and that you love them as you love me."

I am *steaming*. Um – cross, I mean, not smelly.

I have just come home from this church meeting in which one person constantly, relentlessly, at every opportunity relevant or completely irrelevant, keeps sniping and digging at Catholics. In this all-Protestant gathering, I guess she considers that part of the household to be fair game.

I rage at Jesus about this for about half an hour. "How can she?" I am almost shouting. His gaze doesn't waver from my face. I can't read his expression. Serious. Impassive. Though to be honest I'm not a hundred per cent focused on reading his expression. I still have things to say. "What does she know about church history? Does she remember the eighteen Carthusian monks martyred in sixteenth-century England for their refusal to accept Henry VIII as supreme head of the Church of England? Seven of them, including John the Prior of the London Charterhouse, were dragged on hurdles through the City of London to an open place of execution at Tyburn, where they were slowly hanged until they were almost dead, then had their genitals cut off, then were cut open and their bowels pulled out, then their bodies cut into four pieces and their heads cut off. By order of the 'head' of the Church of England because of their steadfast faith! In the compost of this barren desert spiritual wilderness did the Church of England grow! Three of them, Humfrey, William, and Sebastian, had stood in prison upright, chained from their necks to their arms, and their legs fettered with locks and chains for thirteen days. Quiet, humble men of prayer, known for their holiness, all! Does she even *know* about these men in England's history?"

I stop, upset, glaring, trembling.

He looks at me.

"I remember them," he says quietly. "I know them. They are my friends."

I pause on these words, but not for long.

"I'm going to tell her!" I persist belligerently. "The very next time she has *anything* to say about the Catholic Church, I'm going to rebuke her remarks in your holy Name and tell her to stop it!"

Jesus smiles. "No, don't do that," he says gently.

I am still glaring at him. "Well you are, by definition, right," I concede, "but I can't see why not."

He reaches across and just with his fingertips touches the back of my hand. This fingerlight touch surprisingly brings me back from the thorny wilderness of rage I am stamping around in to the here and now.

"There is always something underneath goading and defamation that only love can reach," he says. "Opposition doesn't do the trick."

"Says who?" (I haven't entirely simmered down.) "I remember you having some highly provocative things to say to the Pharisees! 'Blind guides', wasn't it? 'Whitewashed tombs?'"

A slight frown creases his brow. "Different circumstances, different measures," he says. "You weren't there. And − you know − I died for them too."

"So what do you think I should do?" I feel a bit deflated now.

He thinks for a minute, looking down at his hands resting on his knees.

"Maybe next time you go to the group," he says softly, "you could go to work on the issue, but attack the thing, not the person. You have the perfect opportunity here to be the bridge between this new friend and your Catholic friends. Love her − make a point of loving her. Sit with her, chat to her, ask her how her week has been, affirm everything you can in what she contributes; look at her with love in your eyes. The divisions in the church have torn my body apart and ripped out its guts as surely as they disembowelled John at Tyburn. Please − please − don't start a new division, a new separation. Hating someone because they hate Catholics, attacking someone because they are attacking someone else, well… it doesn't make it better."

He looks up at me. Gently he says, "What I'd like best, if you can bring yourself to it, is for you to allow my body to be made whole, so far as it lies with you. To love the most objectionable, the most hostile. To re-member my dismembered body. In the sanctum of your heart. In the holy temple of who you are. To establish and hold in place the beautiful vision I had, still have

– that they may be one. That they may be completely one. As I and the Father are one."

He stops abruptly, and to my horror I watch a tear roll down his face, followed by a second one. My Jesus.

"I will do that for you," I say.

Day 44

Maundy Thursday

Genesis 15:5 NIV

He took him outside and said, "Look up at the sky and count the stars – if indeed you can count them."

Matthew 2:2, 9–10 NIV

"Where is the one who has been born king of the Jews? We saw his star when it rose and have come to worship him…"

… and the star they had seen when it rose went ahead of them until it stopped over the place where the child was. When they saw the star, they were overjoyed.

John 13:30 NIV

As soon as Judas had taken the bread, he went out. And it was night.

Mark 15:33 NIV

At noon, darkness came over the whole land until three in the afternoon.

Isaiah 45:3, 7 KJV

And I will give thee the treasures of darkness, and hidden riches of secret places, that thou mayest know that I, the Lord, which call thee by thy name, am the God of Israel…

… I form the light, and create darkness: I make peace, and create evil: I the Lord do all these things.

It's because I hear his voice that I go down. Just on midnight. I've been reading, and I turn out the light, to leave nothing behind me to disturb the sleeping house. So at first, in darkness, blinded by the light I had come from, I can't see. I let my feet feel the stairway and slide my hand along the rail for safety as I go down, but confidence underlies my hesitancy, because I am used to the dark. I know my night vision will come to me well before I am all the way down.

In the thick, quiet, waiting shadows of the hall, shrouding the life-stir of the house with veils of warm silence, alert for a moment, listening, I discern his presence: "Come outside!"

To the day, the night itself is a wilderness. Light sees itself as the adversary of the dark. One must extinguish the other, as long as lights are lit and night remains.

Going slowly, not wanting to stub my toe on forgotten things strewn careless in my path, I make my way to the door. I unlock it. I turn back briefly, groping for the soft throw flung along the back of the sofa. Folding it as a cloak around my shoulders, I leave the house. I draw the door to behind me, so the night air will not steal in and chill our home.

Barefoot on the stone cold of the wet doorstep, I stand looking up at the stars. This, I remember, this wilderness of stars, is the place of great promise and prescience.

These are the stars that gave to Abram his wild hope of a promised child. The dance of these stars formed into the pattern of a language in which wise men discerned good news of the birth of a kingdom. This is the night that Judas knew, the night that engulfed him as he stepped outside the house and shut the door. I, Judas, stand barefoot on the stone cold step, looking up at the stars, shivering. This is the night in which Jesus wept and prayed and pleaded with his God for another way. But there was none; only this sorrow and this destiny and this night of single necessity, the beginning of the healing of the world. This is the darkness that enveloped the noonday.

As David played the silvery, wandering flow of his harp melodies, he made up songs. He sang of the outbreath of God that enlivens every living being, and the inbreath that draws back the soul from the body – the flow-tide, the ebb-tide of life. He sang of the singing stars who are the messengers of life, telling night unto night the wordless message of the purposes of God. This, the *arcana secretorum*, the treasure of darkness, holds the jewel of new beginning, the seed of light. Light seeds on the midnight field of the sky, a scattering sparkle strewn over the wild spaces of absolute darkness, the stars still make known the ways of God, "night after night they reveal knowledge. They have no speech, they use no words; no sound is heard from them. Yet their voice goes out into all the earth, their words to the ends of the world" (Psalm 19:2–4 NIV).

I stand on the cold stone of the doorstep, and I ask him, "What is it they are singing?"

And he tells me, "They are singing of hope; that at the heart of everything is the seed of its opposite. In the darkest night shines still the seed of light, the promise that all will be well. They are singing of courage, of souls who dare to shine out where darkness would overwhelm the land, and be the starlight in every generation. They are singing of rescue; that in his darkest night, if only a man will look up, he will be comforted by guiding light. They sing of wonder, and beauty and spaciousness, and of majesty too. And as well as singing, if you stand and watch them long enough, you will see they are dancing; their sure steps follow the measure of all that must be. Wise men pay heed to the pattern language of stars."

As I take in his words in silence, I look up hungrily. I wish I could touch a star. I wish all the nervous householders would turn off their bulkhead security lights so I could see the stars properly. I wish we had not poured concrete over the wild places and run electric wires through and swapped streetlights for the scintillating wilderness of stars.

Unwillingly, I accept that the night is colder than my feet can stand. I drink in one last gulp of its clear refreshing air, then turn and reach for the door handle. I pause and look back, look up. "Good night," I whisper. "Good night."

Day 45

Good Friday

Luke 23:20–27, 32–35 NIV

Wanting to release Jesus, Pilate appealed to them again. But they kept shouting, "Crucify him! Crucify him!"

For the third time he spoke to them: "Why? What crime has this man committed? I have found in him no grounds for the death penalty. Therefore I will have him punished and then release him."

But with loud shouts they insistently demanded that he be crucified, and their shouts prevailed. So Pilate decided to grant their demand. He released the man who had been thrown into prison for insurrection and murder, the one they asked for, and surrendered Jesus to their will.

As the soldiers led him away, they seized Simon from Cyrene, who was on his way in from the country, and put the cross on him and made him carry it behind Jesus. A large number of people followed him, including women who mourned and wailed for him…

… Two other men, both criminals, were also led out with him to be executed. When they came to the place called the Skull, they crucified him there, along with the criminals – one on his right, the other on his left. Jesus said, "Father, forgive them, for they do not know what they are doing." And they divided up his clothes by casting lots.

The people stood watching…

This is it, then.

I am still hungry for more time with him, but the story is ending. It is over, and what will happen now? I still have so many questions, there is so much still unsettled in my heart.

"Don't die, Jesus," I whisper. "Please don't die. I didn't… I never… I haven't found out the thing I wanted to know most of all… I needed to ask you… what do you think of me?"

And it seems so awful, in that moment – so self-absorbed and narcissistic – to bring that question up. I expect you agree.

But Jesus… as soon as I whisper the words, somehow he hears me. I can't explain how I see it or what happens, because he does not turn his head. How could he turn his head? He has a cap of stuff like Sussex gorse, with its long, lacerating thorns, jammed down onto it. His arms wrenched back and his wrists nailed hard to the wood, his chest heaving in great breaths of agony, his head already rests back against the cruelty of the thorns. No, he doesn't turn his head.

All I know is, somehow I can suddenly see his face. Dust and blood and tears and sweat all mingling there. His right eye is swollen and so are his lips. Under all the mess and the tangling locks of hair, he is very pale. He looks… awful.

Just for a second, I see into his eyes, see his lips frame a faint reply. "I love you," he says.

And then they lift the cross.

He says nothing more after that, except the things you already know: "Truly I tell you, today you will be with me in paradise"… "Woman, behold your son… behold your mother"… "My God, my God, why have you forsaken me?"… "I'm thirsty"… "It is finished"… "Father into your hands I commend my spirit."

And then just stillness. His body slumps, no longer struggling, just hanging from the nails.

After a while I go home.

What am I to do with that 'I love you'? What am I to understand by it?

I wanted to know what he thought of me – and by that I meant, how did he evaluate me. I suppose I was looking for some kind of grade, or an end-of-term report. I wanted a one-on-one appraisal process. I mean, to be frank, I could guess at a lot of it myself from what I already know of him. When I grumble and complain, when I mock and criticize, I am one hundred per cent sure he would have no time for that at all; that's easy. But there are harder things to evaluate, things that still puzzle me. My divorce, for example. Whose fault was that? I thought I did my best, but – well, did I? My attitude to the church is another. I find most sermons and Bible studies and theological books so excruciatingly boring. Is that because they are, or because I'm shallow and not applying myself properly? I hoped he could tell me. And then there are some things I think might be part of my spiritual path, but might not be – like diet and exercise, making the best of myself. What does he think of that? What does he think of my weakness for ice cream and chocolate? Does it matter, or not at all? Is it okay to eat chocolate that wasn't fairly traded, if I can only afford the little chocolate treats they sell by the checkout? All these things I hoped he'd be able to tell me, weigh my life in the balance and help me fill out a self-appraisal sheet so I'd know what to work on and what things I didn't have to bother about. But all he said was, "I love you."

And why does he love me? Does he love me because of the good things I've done, because of the bits of me that are loveable – like, I am fairly trustworthy and most of the time I tell the truth? Or does he love me like he loved Judas – because someone has to, and because I so, so need him to. That would be loving me, then, *in spite of* what I am.

Or does he love me just unconditionally? Faithfully. Love

like a rock. Love that on the one hand sees through all my pretences, but on the other hand (and maybe for that very reason) asks no questions.

Day 46

Holy Saturday

John 6:12

"Gather the pieces that are left over. Let nothing be wasted." (NIV)
"Gather up the fragments that remain, that nothing be lost." (KJV)
"Gather the pieces left over; let us not waste a bit." (GNT)

Anything to which the word "my" can be attached may be lost – my good looks, my courage, my money, my job, my home, my sanity, my life, my marriage, my integrity, my faith, my power to hold on. Anything. The carrion crow swoops down with its swift flapping wings and plucks it from the hands that held it, whether they were clutching with fearful anxiety or holding it loose with the nonchalance of something that would be "mine" forever. And I do mean *anything*. Jesus, hanging on the cross – would you not have thought he had already given up everything? – also faces the unexpectedness of loss: "My God, my God, why have you forsaken me?" *Anything* to which the word "my" can be attached may be lost. Dashed to pieces.

After it, shorn and bereft, there is the time of waiting. This too is wilderness. Wandering in the wasteland. Forty years in the desert travelling with fluctuating hope sometimes towards and sometimes away from a Promised Land, nomads in tents. Or forty days and nights keeping company with wild beasts and angels, looking hungrily at rocks and arguing with a tempter. Or walking the black dog of depression through the dry lands, accepting that this too will pass – or maybe not. Or filling out form after form and going to interview after interview when the job you thought was certain evaporates. Or the time of explaining to each enquirer, "Actually, she left me." Or the time of waiting in a hospital bed, with the needle inserted ready in the back of your hand, for them to drip into your veins the chemical that must not otherwise touch your skin because it would burn you.

The wilderness is populated with hungry pariahs, and all of them walk alone, looking hopefully at the rocks, wondering if they could possibly be turned into something else. Or not. Above all else, the wilderness holds no certainties. It is a stern place. Its austerity includes no assurances. There is only the waiting, and the wandering, watching for what may emerge, and resisting – if you can – the temptations to chase mirages and grasp at shadows that will be held out to you.

In this case wilderness is the steepest gorge vanishing into darkness unplumbed. Jesus goes alone to harrow hell, to join up life and death. With hindsight it will emerge that his going makes the connection that will hold the pattern of life for all eternity – he makes of his cross the crossing that secures darkness and light into unity. And while the web of life is healed and restored, the pattern drawn again, his body lies dead in the tomb. It is waiting for tomorrow morning, but how can a dead body know it is waiting? How can a dead body know anything? That is how it is with wilderness.

In this day of no-thing I know myself in wilderness; like the depths of the year the ancient Celts called no-time, when the rhythms of life descended into the darkness and the farmers waited for Yul, the turning of the year with the birth of the infant light. An intensity of loneliness possesses my soul. Neither I nor the time has purpose now. I simply am. This is the effect of wilderness. It takes away everything except the I am. For this reason it is essential to making us whole.

Watching for what will emerge from the waiting's womb, the words of Jesus return to me, "Gather up all the pieces that are left, so that nothing is just lost and wasted."

Out of the shreds of a torn life, the new will begin. The shards of the old will be useful for the hardcore underlying the new path to be laid.

Did I ever tell you? The night my youngest child was conceived, I had a vision. In a place of darkness I saw a rosehip, still held aloft on its stem. Hard, its dry sepals fringing the top. Then light began to irradiate it, until it pulsed with light, until its glow spread from the inner intensity to dispel all the darkness around it like the golden glow from an olive oil lamp. And with the coming of the light, the rosehip transformed and became a new rosebud, the sepals once more green and living, protecting the folded petals within. A new time of waiting had begun.

So now, the grave. In the darkness, hidden from sight, the intimate conception of something new begins. The broken body of Jesus is the only shard remaining from the life he had – all that hope, all those miracles, the wonder, the laughter, the healing. Just this broken body. Dead now. God stoops down and gathers up this one broken piece left over, so that nothing of it all may be wasted, nothing be lost.

Life always arrives as infant light in a hidden place of darkness. For a moment, as the word is given, "Let there be light," things retain their unity. Then issues the multiplicity of developing form, the burgeoning of new. That eternal moment, when the Spirit broods over the face of the waters, reveals the waiting in the wilderness as gestation. What we call "my life" is no more than the fleeting instant between the outbreath and the inbreath of God. Of course it is lost, dispersed – "my life" with all the little accoutrements it gathered around it. But Life is not lost, only the form I knew.

This day, Holy Saturday, I do not know all this. Jesus is dead, and I am numb, bereft of all feeling. I do not even understand that I am waiting. I am ~~waiting~~. No. Just I am.

Day 47

Easter Day

Luke 17:20–21 NIV

(using alternative "within you" given to "in your midst")

"The coming of the kingdom of God is not something that can be observed, nor will people say, 'Here it is,' or 'There it is,' because the kingdom of God is within you."

It's Easter Day and I should be feeling happy.

I walk down the steps into the park. That's the way I go to chapel. If you sit in our kitchen, in the right place on the bench by the meal-table, you can look out of the back window and see, rising above the dying honeysuckle hedge and in the clear space of blue above the valley with its trees, the pale stone spire of our chapel pointing to heaven. So to get there, we walk along our road, down the concrete steps, then further down still along the narrow path lined with brambles and sycamores, bindweed and small overhanging trees and shrubs from adjacent gardens. We have to watch our step a bit on that path, because it's where dogs are let off the lead on their morning walk, sometimes with urgent needs to fulfil! There is a bin, but sometimes... At the end of the path the land slopes down again to the duck pond, then the path rises up the other side of the valley. And our chapel is right there.

As I climb the steep path up the far side of the valley, past the ancient chestnut tree with its scars and knobbles, its spreading branches and sprouting children held close, my heart is heavy.

Will I never see him again? I've grown used to seeing that familiar figure, the robe, the sandals, just like I imagined him. Without his stillness, how can I relax? Without his wisdom, how will I know what to do? Without his smile, how will I know not to take myself so seriously? What will be the point of anything, without his company?

I don't know what to do with the incongruity that I am more comfortable with Good Friday than with Easter Day. For all its unspeakable violence, the day of Jesus on the cross is easier for me to find my way into than the incomprehensibility of Jesus risen. His tears, his pain, his terror – even, dare I confess it, his steep climb of forgiveness – I know these things, know what they are. But I do not really understand what it means to pass through the body, right through the door of life and into death's mystery *and then back again*. What is Jesus, risen? Who is Jesus risen? Just the same? Surely not. And, most important for me – *where* is Jesus risen?

In the chapel, we sing the Easter hymns with their notes scaling up like fireworks to shower down from heights of joy.

We settle in our pews to hear the reader. She finds her place in the 24th chapter of Luke's Gospel, tells us she is reading from the NIV, and she sets off. The words "Why do you look for the living among the dead? He is not here; he has risen!" find their way into me. "He is not here." It feels as though I am back to the beginning again. This is my whole problem. How to escape from the map of life that nails me uncompromisingly with its "YOU ARE HERE" to where I am, when he has gone somewhere else? I need a new map, with "YOU TOO ARE SOMEWHERE ELSE" written on it. If I am here and he is not, how can I find him?

Before, I knew at least where to search, because I know what wilderness is. Like Brer Rabbit, I was *born* in the briar patch. I wander nonchalantly through the landscapes of confusion, inadequacy, depression, and grief. Bewilderness has been my home since forever. But I tell you frankly and hope you will not be disappointed – I do not know how to rise.

The service goes on around me, and I ponder this. I am familiar with the Gospels. I know what they say. They are written for and from budding faith communities, and they train the eye to focus on the new. When Luke writes, "Why do you look for the living among the dead?" he redirects our gaze from the world of religious tradition to the new community breaking open among them. When John shows us Thomas present or not present among the gathering of the faithful, and meeting Jesus there when he troubles himself to show up, he is pointing us to the risen Jesus found in the community of faith. But this is an extravert's Gospel. What is there for the cats that walk alone? Bluntly, where am *I* going to find him?

I leave the church with my heart as cold as a stone at night rolled across the entrance of a cave. And when I think of this, the music of a whisper starts up inside me, the familiar stirring of incredulous half-believing joy. "Roll away the stone. Be where life is. The kingdom of God is within you. Stop blocking it."

And I see where I was going wrong. The life and death and rising of Jesus belongs, in one aspect, to history – and to that extent it is outside me. But because I too am part of history, the story lives also in me.

I allow the stone to roll away. I let life emerge in my soul. Right there on the path I stop and reconnect with the living. Above me the pageant of cloudships. Around me the singing of birds. The smell of plants in the rain here in the park. The patterns of tree bark, the sharp green of short spears of new grass. The tossing flight of seagulls against the wild sky. The freshness of the air. I let myself out of the cave of my self-absorbed preoccupations and come out here where life is. I can do this. I can leave the deadness of self behind, and come out into life.

And here in the joy of really seeing, really being, I can touch him again.

Because

Jesus

is

alive.

Afterword

So – did Pen Wilcock really meet Jesus? Did she really walk with him and talk with him and find him in her own Bewilderness in the streets of St Leonards-on-Sea in East Sussex? I mean – is this book *true*?

Yes, she did really meet him, and every day she really walks with him and talks with him, and it really does make all the difference to everything. You should try it for yourself.

But it may help to remember that Pen Wilcock is a writer of fiction, and she finds him in her daily metier. This book is certainly fiction – Pen Wilcock has never worked in a factory on the industrial estate, her neighbours in her present home do not have bulk-head security lights that keep her awake at night or scream at their children, and all the people in her church are friendly and nice. As a matter of fact she feels blessed to be surrounded by the kindest, gentlest people imaginable.

But Jesus is not found only here or there, in this place or that. You do not need to come to St Leonards to look for him. Search in your own Bewilderness, ask him your own questions. It's like he said – "within you".